adults. Differentiating the training needs of part-time from full-time instructors, the authors identify the competencies required of part-time instructors; discuss the various roles and functions of paraprofessionals and offer a systematic way of both planning training programs for paraprofessionals and evaluating their effectiveness; and explain how assessing volunteers' motivations can help educators select appropriate group and individual training techniques and implement effective volunteer training programs.

Programming and instruction in continuing professional education are considered next, and several approaches that emphasize self-directed learning are presented. The book concludes with an analysis of the training function in business and industry. The authors explain how to choose an approach commensurate with particular organizational goals; examine specific functions of training (such as supervisory development and skills training); and outline a step-by-step training process that can be adapted to each function. All those involved in preparing educators of adults and conducting training programs for adults will find this book of value.

THE AUTHORS

STANLEY M. GRABOWSKI is director of continuing education at Boston University.

The other authors are identified in the front of the book.

A publication in
The Adult Education Association
Handbook Series in Adult Education

Preparing
Educators
of Adults

Stanley M. Grabowski
and Associates

Preparing
Educators
of Adults

Jossey-Bass Publishers

San Francisco • Washington • London • 1981

PREPARING EDUCATORS OF ADULTS
by Stanley M. Grabowski and Associates

Copyright © 1981 by: Adult Education Association
of the United States of America
810 Eighteenth Street, N.W.
Washington, D.C. 20006

Jossey-Bass Inc., Publishers
433 California Street
San Francisco, California 94104

Jossey-Bass Limited
28 Banner Street
London EC1Y 8QE

Library of Congress Cataloging in Publication Data

Grabowski, Stanley M.
        Preparing educators of adults.

        Bibliography: p.
        Includes index.
        Contents: Preservice training for instructors
for adults / Phyllis A. Caldwell — Graduate degree
programs for professional adult educators / Roy J.
Ingham, Gardner Hanks — Training part-time
instructional staff / Donald W. Mocker, Elizabeth
Noble — [etc.]
        1. Adult education teachers—Training of—Ad-
dresses, essays, lectures. I. Title.
LC5225.T4G7   371.1'22   80-1104
ISBN 0-87589-509-3   AACR2

Manufactured in the United States of America

JACKET DESIGN BY WILLI BAUM

FIRST EDITION

Code 8123

The AEA Handbook Series in Adult Education

WILLIAM S. GRIFFITH

University of British Columbia

HOWARD Y. McCLUSKY

University of Michigan

General Editors

Edgar J. Boone
Ronald W. Shearon
Estelle E. White
and Associates
Serving Personal and
Community Needs Through
Adult Education

April 1980

Huey B. Long
Roger Hiemstra
and Associates
Changing Approaches
to Studying Adult
Education

April 1980

John M. Peters
and Associates
Building an Effective
Adult Education
Enterprise

April 1980

Alan B. Knox
and Associates
Developing, Administering,
and Evaluating
Adult Education

October 1980

Robert D. Boyd
Jerold W. Apps
and Associates
Redefining
the Discipline
of Adult Education

October 1980

Alexander N. Charters
and Associates
Comparing
Adult Education
Worldwide

March 1981

Burton W. Kreitlow
and Associates
Examining Controversies
in Adult Education

March 1981

Stanley M. Grabowski
and Associates
Preparing Educators
of Adults

October 1981

Foreword

Adult education as a field of study and practice is not well understood by many literate and intelligent American adults whose exposure to the field has been limited to one or a few aspects of its apparently bewildering mosaic. Since 1926, when the American Association for Adult Education (AAAE) was founded, the leaders of that organization and those of its successor, the Adult Education Association of the U.S.A. (AEA), have striven to communicate to both the neophytes in the field and the adult public an understanding of its diverse and complex enterprises. A major vehicle for accomplishing this communication has been a sequence of handbooks of adult education, issued periodically to convey a broad view of the mosaic. In 1934, 1936, and 1948 the AAAE published the first three handbooks. Although the Association had intended to issue a handbook every two years, the plan was not carried out for a number of reasons, including the outbreak of World War II and the termination of financial support by the Carnegie Corporation. Within three years of the publication of the 1948 handbook the Association dissolved itself in order to establish the AEA, which included the former members of both the AAAE and the Department of Adult Education of the National Edu-

cation Association. It was nine years before the AEA was able
to publish its first handbook, the fourth in the sequence, followed a decade later by the fifth version.

In the early 1970s both the Publications Committee of
AEA and the Commission of the Professors of Adult Education (an affiliated organization of the AEA) explored the
kinds of handbooks that could be designed to serve the changing nature and needs of the field. They found that different
parts of the field were developing at different rates—in some
areas information was becoming outdated rapidly, whereas in
others a decennial handbook would be adequate to maintain
currency. Moreover, the growing literature and the many developments in policies and programs led them to conclude
that a single volume of traditional size would not be sufficient
to treat the expanding knowledge base, the changing policies
and practices, and the controversial topics in adult education.
Accordingly, the Publications Committee decided that the next
handbook would consist of several volumes, allowing the presentation of an increased amount of information on each of
eight selected parts of the field, and preparing the way for sub-
sequent revisions of each volume independently on a schedule
reflecting the pace of change in each area. The result is The
AEA Handbook Series in Adult Education, which has been developed by the general editors with the guidance and assistance
of the Publications Committee.

In this volume in the AEA Handbook Series the authors
have sought to present two aspects of training. The first deals
with the professional graduate preparation, or in some cases upgrading, of individuals who are engaged in the practice of adult
education as administrators, part-time or full-time teachers,
paraprofessionals, or volunteers. The second involves the full
range of training programs conducted by adult educators, from
the continuing professional education of those holding professional degrees, licenses, or other certificates to the most elementary of educational programs for laborers with little formal previous education. Unlike other publications dealing with the
preparation of adult educators or the practice of training in
specific settings, this book neither debates the relative merits of

the contributions of selected disciplines to the preparation of professional adult educators nor pontificates about assumed differences between education and training. Rather, it examines, describes, and analyzes both training programs for adult educators and training programs adult educators conduct.

Descriptive surveys of the university degree programs for training adult educators have been conducted at irregular intervals since the mid fifties. Although they vary in breadth and depth, no previous report of such a survey both describes and prescribes the nature of a design process for the construction of an appropriate curriculum for preparing professional adult educators as agents of change. In this book a design schema is proposed, one which has the appearance of being logically designed and which may offer professors of adult education in particular and professors of other education specialties as well a new and useful way of improving the effectiveness of their curricula.

Adult education teachers historically have moved into their positions on either a full-time or part-time basis on the strength of their academic preparation in some disciplinary area. Only after they have been teaching adults for some time and have reflected on their experience do they become aware of the field of study known as adult education, and then some choose to pursue formal training to help them perform more effectively in the positions they already occupy. With the increase in the number of career teaching positions and a growing awareness of adult education as a field of university study on the part of administrators who hire teachers of adults has come a concomitant expansion in the number of persons seeking preservice training to prepare themselves for their chosen field. Readers of this book will gain both an overview of the development of this aspect of training and a preview of its future.

Much of the teaching of adults continues to be conducted by part-time teachers, paraprofessionals, and volunteers. Although the full-time teachers and administrators are much more conspicuous and tend to receive a disproportionately larger share of public attention than do the part-timers, paraprofessionals, and volunteers, a proper balance, reflecting their contributions to the work of training, is demonstrated in this book.

In the last three chapters the focus shifts from the preparation of trainers of various kinds to the training functions performed in business and industrial organizations. Although not all of the authors in this section elected to use the phrase "human resources development," it is clear that they agree concerning the humanistic yet practical goals which training must serve.

Preparing Educators of Adults was intended to present the thesis that adult education and training are so closely related that those who see themselves working in one area but not the other would be able to advance their chosen field by acknowledging their kinship and joining forces to further their common goals. It presents clearly and concisely both a perspective on the preparation of trainers and an overview of the programs trainers conduct. The other seven volumes in the AEA Handbook Series in Adult Education deal with Serving Personal and Community Needs through Adult Education; Building an Effective Adult Education Enterprise; Changing Approaches to Studying Adult Education; Redefining the Discipline of Adult Education; Developing, Administering, and Evaluating Adult Education; Examining Controversies in Adult Education; and Comparing Adult Education Worldwide.

The preparation of the series involved the cooperation and dedicated efforts of scores of chapter authors, volume organizers, Publication Committee members, and successive executive committees of the AEA. It is appropriate to single out for recognition the chairmen of the Publications Committee who have been intimately involved in the production of this series since the inception of the idea: Beverly B. Cassara, Jerold W. Apps, James A. Farmer, Jr., Allen B. Moore, Harold Rose, and Carole Kasworm. Their never-failing support and encouragement were essential in carrying out this attempt to communicate an understanding and appreciation of adult education to workers in this field and to other literate and intelligent adults whose view of the field has been limited.

August 1981   WILLIAM S. GRIFFITH

HOWARD Y. MCCLUSKY

General Editors

Preface

This book presents an up-to-date overview of training in various settings. Training is here defined to include all kinds of personnel development, both skill training in the narrow sense and education in the wider sense; training encompasses the individual parts as well as the whole of what has become known as human resources development.

Training activities are used to prepare personnel at all levels and under diverse kinds of institutional sponsorship. Training is used in business and industry as well as in governmental, military, educational, voluntary, and proprietary agencies, institutions, and organizations. The preparation of instructors and professors of adult and continuing education is also part of training. Whatever the setting, whatever the methodology, whoever the recipients, training is concerned with behavioral change.

There are some basic competencies that every trainer of adults ought to possess; the literature on this topic is relatively rich and does not need repetition here. The relative emphasis placed on each of the competencies varies among specific professions and vocations. Various criteria are employed in determining the appropriate emphasis for each. Some of these criteria are considered in this volume.

Most individuals concerned with training are already familiar with the basic models used in training. Such models are reported, explained, demonstrated, and applied in numerous sources. They are not presented here in generic fashion, but are mentioned by some of the authors in discussions of specific practices. For the most part, the authors use such models as their point of departure. Most of the authors address three major areas in their chapters: the state of the art, the ideal training program for the specific clientele under consideration, and the implementation of such a program.

Readers who want detailed information about practices and procedures are referred to the American Society for Training and Development's handbook, *Training and Development Handbook: A Guide to Human Resource Development* (2nd ed.), edited by Robert L. Craig.

Training has suffered from an anti-intellectualism; it has been noted for its lack of research and its abundance of pragmatism and practicality. The lack of an intellectual base kept the practice a craft and prevented its becoming a profession. An attempt to transform it into a profession resting on theoretical bases has occurred only in recent years. The development and proliferation of graduate programs in the field have contributed immensely toward establishing training as a profession based on research and theoretical knowledge. This volume is intended to contribute toward that end, while offering readers up-to-date information on recent developments and trends.

In Chapter One, Phyllis Caldwell reviews the literature concerning the preservice training of adult educators, concentrating on the competencies of adult education administrators and teachers. She describes several training models and cites examples of actual programs using some variations of those models. She closes with a prescription for practitioners on developing a preservice training program.

In Chapter Two, Roy Ingham and Gardner Hanks trace the history of graduate studies in adult education as a background for their presentation of an ideal curriculum and its application to adult education. They offer a Method of Designing Action Systems (MODAS) and, for each of its twelve steps, they discuss the function, provide criteria for evaluation, suggest teaching approaches, and consider methodological difficulties. They conclude with suggestions on the use of MODAS in practice and its implications for organizing instruction.

In Chapter Three, Donald Mocker and Elizabeth Noble address the training of part-time adult education teachers, arguing that part-time personnel require a different pattern of training from full-time personnel. They list twenty-four competencies as a guide for the development of part-time teachers.

In Chapter Four, Bettie Lee Yerka briefly notes the emergence of the paraprofessional movement, the issues relative to paraprofessionalism, the role and characteristics of paraprofessionals, and patterns of paraprofessional utilization. She proposes a systematic approach to the choice of a training plan and recommends training for both paraprofessional and professional staff members. She concludes with an assessment of paraprofessionals' effectiveness and a look at implications for the future.

In Chapter Five, Stephen Confer describes present practices for the training of volunteers and proposes two hypotheses: volunteers tend to be more sociocentric than egocentric, and volunteers tend to prefer training programs that emphasize group activity. He discusses the need to develop training styles appropriate to volunteers' own values, goals, and needs, and he suggests techniques most applicable for training volunteers. He concludes with a proposal for an ideal training program and its implementation.

In Chapter Six, Stanley Grabowski examines continuing education for the professions. He defines the need for and purpose of continuing education for professionals, noting that mandatory continuing education is now a controversial issue. He explains how different providers make their offerings available and argues strongly for a greater emphasis on self-directed learning. He concludes by identifying those characteristics that ought to guide continuing education activities for professionals.

In Chapter Seven, Irwin Jahns examines the training function within organizations. He notes the reasons for the negative image of training and offers a synthesis and integration of the central tendencies involved in training, education, staff development, and organizational development. He shows how the training process relates to other organizational systems and how it influences stability and change. He presents alternative models for training systems and raises questions to help readers think through the analysis and integration of various training systems.

In Chapter Eight, Stephen Becker classifies the training in business and industry using six categories: organizational development, management and executive development, supervisory development, sales training, technical-professional training, and skills training. He identifies ten steps in the training process and ends with a statement about the emergence of human resources development.

In Chapter Nine, Don Seaman and Donnie Dutton discuss the opportunities for human resources development. They report data relating to the size and scope of training in business and industry, in the federal goverment, in the military, and in government-sponsored work and training programs. Their final statement deals with the challenges of the future and they identify eight trends for the years ahead.

In the Postscript, a review of the major themes treated in the preceding nine chapters is presented. After acknowledging the myriad factors that tend to make the field of training appear to be composed of disparate, unrelated areas of practice, the author proposes that progress for those engaged in all aspects of the field ultimately depends on the willingness of volunteers, paraprofessionals, part-time and full-time trainers, and adult educators to recognize that they are all engaged in a common field of work.

Boston, Massachusetts   STANLEY M. GRABOWSKI
August 1981

Contents

The Authors

STEPHEN P. BECKER, president, LEARNCOM

PHYLLIS A. CALDWELL, vice-president for personnel, Arkwright-Boston Insurance

STEPHEN H. CONFER, administrative assistant to the president and director of employment programs, Communication Workers of America

DONNIE DUTTON, professor, Adult Education Program, University of Arkansas

STANLEY M. GRABOWSKI, professor, School of Education, Boston University

GARDNER HANKS, director, Albia Public Library

ROY J. INGHAM, associate professor, College of Education, Florida State University

IRWIN R. JAHNS, associate professor, College of Education, Florida State University

DONALD W. MOCKER, professor, School of Education, University of Missouri–Kansas City

ELIZABETH NOBLE, assistant professor, School of Education, University of Missouri–Kansas City

DONALD F. SEAMAN, professor, Adult Education Program, Texas A & M University

BETTIE LEE YERKA, associate professor and program coordinator, Cooperative Extension, Cornell University

xix

Preparing
Educators
of Adults

Chapter One

Preservice Training
for Instructors
of Adults

Phyllis A. Caldwell

Preservice training for practitioners of adult education is a relatively recent concern in the field. The recent phenomenal growth of adult education has stimulated the need for trained teachers, both full and part time. The training needs for several adult education roles and specializations have been identified, and considerable concern over the competencies for adult education teachers has been expressed. Yet, although many preservice training models have been proposed, no evidence has been presented to demonstrate the superiority of any one model, in large part because of the lack of clearly defined and implemented evaluation procedures. Substantial research on preservice training programs must be conducted to identify models suitable for replication that will provide high quality training for the growing number of professionals in adult education. In this chapter, I review the literature on preservice training, examine present models, and propose a prescription for practitioners.

Review of the Literature

A comprehensive review of the literature concerning the training of adult educators reveals that although considerable investigation has been undertaken, there have been few conclusive findings. An investigation of training literature reveals four main topics of concentration: the rationale and need for training adult education personnel, the identification of personnel who require training, the training requirements of diverse specialists within adult education, and the need for competency-based training of personnel.

The last decade witnessed a dramatic increase in the number of adults engaging in educational pursuits and in the number and diversity of settings in which these activities occur. Literacy training and life skills education, now viewed as vital to the survival of American society, have received support from the federal government and numerous other public agencies. The need for training and retaining workers has prompted the development of educational programs in the industrial sector. Leisure pursuits, enrichment activities, and nontraditional activities are expanding in postsecondary institutions. Professional associations and businesses are promoting continuing professional education for their members and employees.

Within these varied settings, numerous individuals may be appropriately termed adult educators. Houle (1970) describes the specializations and reporting relationships in the field of adult education as resembling the general shape of a pyramid. Divided horizontally into three levels, the pyramid has as its base the largest group of people, those who serve as volunteers. At the intermediate level of the pyramid, Houle identifies a smaller group of people who, as part of their paid employment, combine adult education functions with other responsibilities. The smallest group of people at the apex of the pyramid are the full-time specialists whose primary concern and occupation is adult education.

The unprecedented recent growth of adult education places yet greater demands on the limited number of already overworked career professionals in the field. Until recently, the majority of those responsible for the education of adults were volunteers and part-time workers under the direction of the full-time specialists in adult education. Volunteers and part-time adult educators are largely self-taught, acquiring their skill and expertise through on-the-job learning. Whatever training in adult education they receive is acquired during in-service programs.

The recent growth and changing demands in the field of adult education indicate that a largely self-taught, part-time, and volunteer staff will not suffice. Verner and others (1970) document the emergence of a professional group of adult educators to respond to societal needs for continuous learning in a complicated and highly dynamic environment. The education of adults once directed by volunteers is increasingly the responsibility of specialists.

Adult education as a profession is correctly seen as interdisciplinary. Yet, as the field continues to emerge and grow, it is evident that a unique body of knowledge, not included in other disciplines, can be said to characterize the field. Douglah and Moss (1969) include in this unique body of knowledge "the history and philosophy of adult education; the study of how adults learn, and the investigation of factors which facilitate or impede the learning process; the study of the motivational factors which prompt an adult to seek out educational opportunities; the investigation of the area of instruction, including the study of what methods are most appropriate for disseminating knowledge, developing skills, and changing attitudes" (p. 129).

Schroeder and Haggerty (1976) summarize the principles of a staff development program designed to train specialists for a learner-centered, rather than a teacher-centered, environment with consideration of the unique needs and characteristics of adult learners. DeSanctis (1976) identifies the overriding requirement of preservice and in-service training as the preparation of teachers for a learner-centered environment, as opposed to a teacher-centered environment.

Douglah and Moss (1969) identify several professional roles in adult education by considering how various professionals

apply the content of the field. Each role has its own professional preparation and training needs. For example, the adult education researcher or professor requires graduate training with emphasis on adult education as a field, research methodology, and
theory development. The training needs of adult education administrators, counselors, consultants, and program designers include work in organizing, administering, and supervising adult
education institutions and personnel. Teachers of adults, whose
prime focus lies in another profession or a specialized subject
area, need training in adult education methods, adult learning,
and the design of appropriate instructional activities. Most
teachers of adults in professional continuing education have indepth knowledge and experience with the content of a specialized field but little preparation in the design of appropriate
learning situations for adults.

Special training needs have been most critically examined
in specialized areas of adult education like adult basic education
(ABE) and cooperative extension (Verner and others, 1970).
The University of Missouri (1973) conducted a nationwide survey of ABE teachers to determine what sorts of additional training they considered useful. Training needs identified by this survey include: training in effective teaching procedures; visiting
other teachers to observe successful techniques; training in how
to relate to students; courses to increase knowledge of subject
matter; training that addresses the problems of individual teachers; and training in materials preparation.

A survey of New England ABE teachers (Curriculum Research and Development Center of the University of Rhode Island, 1975) was conducted to identify areas for preservice training. Areas identified by teachers as being "definitely necessary"
include preservice training in: teaching reading and English as a
second language; individualizing instruction; applying adult
learning theory; identifying and using new materials; understanding learning disabilities; diagnosing needs and evaluating
students; and placing and orienting students.

Whitlock (1967) reviewed the education and training of
industrial trainers and staff development specialists who were
members of the American Society of Training and Develop-

ment. Whitlock reports that the majority of the respondents received no formal training for the position. The respondents described their preparation as "self-taught" and "on-the-job experience." Understanding the need for formal preservice training, the respondents indicated that they would give their staffs more specific training than that which they themselves had received, including company courses or training, conference leadership, college courses, seminars, and personal coaching.

Much of the literature on adult educator training seeks to identify the competencies of adult education teachers and administrators. Chamberlain (1961) thoroughly investigated the essential competencies (knowledge, skills, and attitudes) that adult educators need to be considered professionally competent. The most frequently mentioned competencies, as rated by adult education professors, students enrolled in graduate education programs, and institutional administrators, were: communication skills, program development, administrative skills, and knowledge of the principles of adult education.

Mocker (1974) worked extensively in defining the competencies necessary for ABE teachers. Using the Adult Basic Education Competency Inventory, he refined a list of 200 ranked competencies systematically classified into three categories: knowledge, behavior, and attitudes. Four major competency areas are: scope and goal of adult education, curriculum, ABE learner, and instructional process. The competency inventory has been used for staff development efforts in several states.

To identify the necessary competencies of adult education administrators and adult basic education instructors, Smith (1977) employed a modification of the Delphi technique. A group of sixteen adult education administrators from the state of Iowa selected a final list of 167 administrator competencies. At the same time, another group of administrators and instructors selected 136 ABE teacher competencies. All panel participants were asked to identify when individuals should attain the competency: prior to entering the field of adult education, at the beginning of their work in adult education, or at a later stage in their career.

Bunning (1976), investigating the skills and knowledge

requisite for adult educators, found that no study had addressed itself specifically to the needs of future adult educators. Employing the Delphi technique, Bunning sampled 141 professors of adult education, asking them to predict the skills and knowledge that future adult educators would need to perform their jobs adequately and to suggest the most appropriate learning experiences for attaining such skills and knowledge. He organized the highest-rated skills and knowledge into six general categories representing adult educator functions: the adult educator himself, the field of adult education, the adult learner, the adult education environment, adult education programming, and the adult education process.

Grabowski (1976), after substantial review of the competencies in several studies, distilled ten competencies that are common to most studies. The competent adult educator:

1. understands and takes into account the motivation and participation patterns of adult learners
2. understands and provides for the needs of adult learners
3. is versed in the theory and practice of adult learners
4. knows the community and its needs
5. knows how to use various methods and techniques of instruction
6. possesses communication and listening skills
7. knows how to locate and use education materials
8. has an open mind and allows adults to pursue their own interests
9. continues his or her own education
10. is able to evaluate and appraise a program

The American Society for Training and Development conducted a study to identify the basic skills, knowledge, and abilities required for effective performance in training and development ("Important New ASTD Study . . . ," 1977). Instruments were designed to survey a representative sample of the society's members and determine a listing of weighted competencies that would provide a basis for professional development through human resources training programs for professionals. Several other studies regarding requisite competencies for adult education teachers and administrators seem to agree with Smith (1977), who notes that "It is relatively easy to develop lists of competencies but very time consuming and expensive to develop the training and evaluation packages based on these competencies" (p. 21).

The establishment of competency-based training programs leading to adult education teacher certification has recently become a much discussed issue, both as the possible logical terminal point of preservice training and as a process that could contribute to the further growth of the profession. For the numerous part-time and marginal employees in public school adult education, certification could provide job security and improved status. However, the complexity of the issue of credentialing becomes evident as one considers the numerous part-time teachers and consultants whose specialties lie in fields other than adult education and whose expertise is sought for credit and noncredit adult education programs.

The Commission of Professors of Adult Education's task force on certification examined adult education certification (Cameron, Rockhill, and Wright, 1976). After discussing the possible positive contributions of certification and the problems connected with a suitable certification system, the task force concluded: "If adult education, as a profession, is to pursue certification and avoid some of its abuses it should begin to: (1) conduct the necessary research on the relation of training to performance and on the effects of performance for the individuals and society; (2) experiment with the design of programs for effective training; (3) provide consultant assistance to groups facing certification issues; (4) promote alternative ways of acquiring competence; and (5) over the long run, train individuals to evaluate services, to know their rights and to demand them, and to become increasingly independent of service institutions" (pp. 10-11).

The literature on preservice training of adult educators provides sparse information and few if any conclusive findings. Areas of concern and problems have been identified in the literature, indicating that much work remains to be done before a

research-based preservice training program for adult education
teachers can be developed.

Models for Preservice Training

A review of the literature reveals that beyond formal university degree programs in adult and continuing education, preservice training programs are not common. Without formal full-
time employment and lifetime career patterns for adult teachers,
training has been an in-service rather than a preservice activity.
On the whole, the search for model training programs has also
yielded disappointing results. Hoffman and Pagano (1976) relate that ABE staff training has been fragmented and uncoordi-
nated. After an intensive study of the training literature and
ABE staff development efforts in thirty-eight states, the Center
for Resource Development in Adult Education at the University
of Missouri-Kansas City (1973) notes that "The most singular
discovery emerging from the nearly eighteen months of study
devoted to this project is how little is known about adult basic
education teacher training by those most closely associated with
it—its supporters, administrators, practitioners, and participants" (University of Missouri, 1973, p. 1). While attempting to
identify models and innovative programs for teacher training,
Grabowski (1976) observed that the criteria originally established for identifying and selecting programs proved to be so
rigorous that no programs were identified.

Verner and others (1970) argue that special academic
preparation is needed to educate adult education leaders. Individuals employed full time with a career commitment to the
field are in need of graduate study. Part-time adult educators
can be served by university courses, workshops, and other in-
service activities. The training needs of volunteer workers can be
met by in-service programs conducted by those professionally
trained in the field.

Currently available preservice training programs include
graduate school programs, two-year degree-granting programs,
and short workshops. To date, graduate programs, especially
those resulting in the Ph.D. or Ed.D. degree, have been intended

to train adult education researchers, university teachers, and continuing education administrators. Only limited data on graduate training programs are available. Grabowski (1976) notes that, according to data supplied by the Commission of Professors of Adult Education, only seventy-five universities in the U.S. have full-time graduate offerings in adult education and about another fifty provide some courses in adult education. Several institutions have initiated professional preservice master's degree programs that combine one year of graduate study with an internship. The emphasis in these programs is on competency-based field-centered preparation.

Some colleges and universities have established resource centers for staff development. The services of a resource center usually include: university courses designed to respond to training needs, field-based courses, consultative and training services provided by professors at the institution, and a library of curriculum materials and media.

Short-term workshops are the most commonly used model for preservice training of volunteer and part-time adult teachers. Often organized before an academic adult education program commences, a preservice training program may be organized by the director of the prospective program, using university professors or outside consultants as resources.

Other training programs are based on an institute model. In an effort to train master teachers, who would in turn prepare other teachers, regional summer institutes in adult basic education have been conducted. Florida State University (1968) organized a regional institute with follow-up activities that provided participants with further technical assistance at the local level. Regional summer institutes emphasize two very broad preparation areas: knowledge of content and experience in specialized teaching techniques. By 1972, under the sponsorship of the U.S. Office of Education, all ten geographical regions defined by the Department of Education had initiated staff development efforts using the institute model.

Not only is there a dearth of preservice training programs for teachers of adults, but also most existing training programs lack an evaluation component. The absence of evaluation procedures constitutes a serious deficiency in training program models. Far too often evaluation of training programs merely consists of questionnaires that elicit the responses of program participants. These questionnaires, or happiness indicators, measure the receptivity or responsiveness of the participants, but fail to measure the mastery of subject matter acquired by the participants or their attainment of program goals.

The Mississippi Institute for Teacher Training in ABE employed pre- and posttest evaluation techniques to measure cognitive change for the participants (Seaman and Kohler, 1969). Because the reliability of the test instrument approached zero, further investigation into the change scores and their interpretation was abandoned.

Training programs for adult basic education teachers are far more numerous than for any other group of adult education teachers. A few experimental preservice programs identify directions for future training activities. Although various training models (including graduate training, workshop training, and institute training) have been examined, a review of these experimental programs leads to the conclusion that very little rigorous research has been done on improving adult education teacher training.

The University of Southern California (1970) conducted a one-year program, with emphasis on training in English as a second language (ESL), to prepare thirty persons to be ABE teachers. Using a competency-based training design, the program provided field experience, coursework, and academic studies within the structure of modular scheduling. Through intensive, well-directed, and supervised field experience, participants directly applied their specialized university training. Students in the program studied several learning modules, all experience-oriented, self-directed, and self-paced. The modules covered methods and directed teaching of ESL (including sixty hours of teaching in an adult school classroom), principles of adult education, development of an adult school curriculum, counseling, sociology of education (including work in community surveys), linguistics, and evaluation. Participant competencies were developed through both specialized academic training and field experience.

Assessments were made frequently during the one-year program using self-evaluation, university evaluation, and field supervisor's evaluation. Ongoing process evaluations conducted by the participants and instructors permitted program and course changes as needed. Instructors evaluated participants' success in completing course objectives and requirements, and videotapes were used for self-evaluation. The attrition rate was low, and participants were successful in earning the California Adult Teaching Credential, obtaining employment, completing the directed teaching experience, and achieving other intended goals. Subjective evaluations by supervisors and by principals within adult schools revealed a favorable opinion of the competencies of the training participants.

The Women's Leadership Project was a one-year training program (1974-75) designed cooperatively by the Boston University School of Education and the State Department to prepare women administrators for adult and continuing education programs (Boston University School of Education, 1975). This competency-based training model combined a field internship in continuing education programs throughout the state and interdepartmental coursework at Boston University. The ten program interns participated in an assessment to identify educational leadership competencies, and each participant used the results to identify individualized objectives and learning experiences. These included a week-long residential seminar followed by a one-year intensive training program with the following components: academic courses at Boston University, fieldwork in administration at selected adult and continuing education sites, ongoing group support seminars, and individually contracted learning programs.

The program participants, university instructors, consultants, and field supervisory personnel all played a part in the continuous evaluation of participant progress and program success. Participant self-assessment was conducted at the onset and conclusion of the training program. Project faculty and field supervisors graded the participants and submitted written evaluations on progress and competencies. The value of the training model would have been substantially enhanced through the use of clearly defined, objective evaluation procedures to complement the self-ratings.

Drawing from participant self-ratings, the final project report notes: "The biggest *change* from the beginning of the program took place overall, in areas which include: knowledge of selected women's issues, organizational theory, personal assessment and planning, decision making, goal setting and long range planning, and evaluation. Particularly notable was the tremendous increase in self-confidence over the year as participants encountered and mastered new situations. Critical here, in addition, was the self-exploration encouraged in group process and other sessions, the support function performed by the group when an individual was having difficulty, and the frequent encounters with women role models, demonstrating that participants' career goals could, in fact, be achieved in reality. This self-confidence is reflected in the long-term goals of students and the types of employment they are now seeking or were able to obtain following the year of training" (Boston University School of Education, 1975, p. 5).

The Proteus Adult Education Research and Development Team of Visalia, California (1969), developed a preservice training model to prepare teachers and teacher aides of Mexican-American students. Materials related to four major training goals (Zinn, 1975): (1) to give the participants an understanding of their motivations for wanting to work in an ABE/ESL program; (2) to give them a thorough understanding of the psychology of the adult learner; (3) to give them a firsthand experience of the difficulties involved in learning another language; and (4) to give them instruction in the techniques and methodology of teaching English as a second language.

This training model covered an initial thirty hours of intensive training over a two-week period followed by weekly three-hour in-service sessions. The training techniques included small group discussions, microlabs, role play, games, and structured lectures. The training effort showed creative training techniques and methods, but unfortunately insufficient emphasis was placed on evaluation to assist trainers interested in designing similar programs or in modifying the Proteus model.

Another relatively short-term preservice training program, Project Homebound in Butte, Montana (Hartstead and Venner, 1970), serviced American-Indian and Mexican-American

ABE students at home by preparing adult education personnel of varied educational backgrounds. Master teachers with college degrees, teacher aides, trainees often without high school diplomas, and volunteers cooperated to supply the home services. During the initial eighteen days, a workshop was offered to prepare trainees lacking previous teaching experience. Using lecture, discussion, and role playing, consultants developed the trainees' skills in communication, special teaching methods for working with the disadvantaged, and adult teaching techniques. The trainees experienced a hands-on approach, using the materials and methods, team teaching, and teaching. The volunteers conducted classes in students' homes, with a teacher present for support. Extensive in-service training by consultants and master teachers continued for the aides and volunteers. In evaluating the training, Hartstead and Venner (1970) report considerable use of the personnel trained by the program, and impressions from supervisory visits revealed that adequate teaching competency had apparently been developed.

At the Southeastern Institute for teacher training in ABE, Florida State University faculty prepared a group of highly selected teacher trainers and master teachers to provide preservice and in-service training for adult basic education teachers and aides in their local settings (Florida State University, 1968). The three-week regional institute provided planning, technical, and instructional assistance for various state and local workshops. Weekly forms completed by participants revealed strengths and weaknesses throughout the institute. Pre- and posttests revealed that fifty-five of the sixty-five participants made some overall gain in mastering both subject matter and content. However, the evaluation indicated that the reported results were limited because the testing instruments were not validated. Follow-up observations of the participants made at state and community workshops indicated that behavioral and attitudinal changes measured through pre- and posttesting were maintained (p. 45).

The University of Chicago's Teacher Training Conference was designed to prepare teachers to work with urban clients (University of Chicago, 1972). The conference had ten major objectives, among which were increasing the participants' ability to identify and to use specific teaching skills and strategies; increasing the participants' ability to analyze their educational setting and to use this analysis to devise, implement, and evaluate educational activities; heightening the participants' awareness of self-directed learning models of instruction and practice in their use; increasing the participants' awareness of black adult learners' experience and of the urban environment. The conference included experiential, analytical, theoretical, practical, and reflective components.

As a self-directed learning model, the conference afforded participants maximum flexibility and an opportunity to develop and pursue their objectives for the conference, to select learning activities to meet those objectives, and to evaluate their progress toward the attainment of those objectives. Thorough conference evaluation procedures, designed mainly to assess the effectiveness of a self-directed learning model, were implemented. Among the questions to be answered by the evaluation were: Is a self-directed learning model acceptable to conferees? Do participants make cognitive gains at the conference? Do supervisors see changes in teachers' behavior following participation in this conference? Will a substantial number of conferees implement a self-directed learning model with their ABE students? Does a two-week conference allow enough time for teachers to comprehend the self-directed model so that they can transfer it?

Conference participants submitted case studies, learning plans, and daily logs. Supervisors evaluated the performance of each conferee prior to the conference and again three months after the conference. Case studies completed by conferees before the conference as well as three months after the conference revealed their cognitive gain and showed that one half of this gain persisted at least three months after the conference. Supervisors reported changes in terms of the specific ways conferees were able to apply their experiences in their home institutions. The final report on the training conference states that the model shows the utility of self-directed learning for short-term ABE training.

An experimental training program to develop a model for ABE in correctional institutions and to provide specialized training to selected individuals in ABE in corrections provided clearly defined and evaluated short-term training (Hawaii University, 1970). A needs assessment survey of correctional institutions determined discrepancies between existing and ideal ABE programs. The training program aims called for the development of knowledge (the philosophy and theory of instruction in ABE; concepts and principles of the ABE learning process; procedures, innovative techniques, and instructional material and media for ABE), skills (model design; writing behavioral objectives; creating learning environments; using federal, state, and community resources), and attitudes (positive feelings toward the concept of ABE; elimination of illiteracy in correctional institutions). Training was evaluated by use of pre- and posttesting and comparisons of posttest scores with criterion standards for acceptable performance. Analysis of the results from criterion tests administered at the close of training indicates that the training program was effective in developing participants' knowledge and skills and in fostering positive attitudes. All but three participants reached criterion standards. Although long-term evaluation is needed to validate the program, a general endorsement of the program design and its replicability is indicated.

To respond to the numerous instructional settings and diverse teaching requirements of adult education, individualized and self-paced training models for adult educators are under development and refinement in two states, Colorado and Florida. Schroeder and Haggerty (1976) describe a nontraditional approach to staff development in Colorado. The adult educator trainee, working in close coordination with a university facilitating organization or resource person, identifies and prioritizes competency needs. Individually tailored learning packages included literary and audiovisual resources, prescribed consultations with experts, visits to adult education programs, and participation in training workshops. The trainee submits ongoing evaluations and reports on the various experiences and sets a training schedule.

Similar to this program, the Consortium of Florida Adult Educators and Practitioners (1976) has designed a performance-based adult educator training program. A self-assessment inventory is conducted based on five categories of competencies—community relations, instructional skills, understanding the learner, interpersonal relationships, and curriculum knowledge and planning. Individualized training experiences are designed to respond to learner needs in each of the five areas. Final evaluations of both the Colorado and Florida programs and recommendations based on these evaluations are not yet available.

Prescription for Practitioners

The diversity of both adult education and the professional careers within it defies the development of a single preservice training program. A model preservice training program for teachers of adults should include: (1) assessment of participant training needs; (2) identification of a specific target group of participants; (3) competency-based training; (4) integration of academic and on-the-job or field experience; (5) individualized training techniques; (6) formative and summative evaluation involving project participants; and (7) evaluation by expert external evaluators.

The context of preservice training can be as important to its success as are its design and implementation. The preservice training models described in this chapter are the result of a cooperative effort among individuals with identified training needs, sponsoring agencies (including universities) that provide training expertise, and state departments of education that provide financial support.

Preservice training programs for adult basic education personnel are frequently reviewed in the literature. Both the acute need for training in this specialized area and the availability of federal funding for training have encouraged programs for this group of adult educators. Training for individuals who are instructors in professional continuing education programs and in postsecondary credit and noncredit programs is equally important, though not eligible for special funding. Appropriate and exemplary preservice training accompanied by thorough research and evaluation is needed to develop the adult teachers whose expertise is critical to the continued growth and legitimacy of the field of adult education and to the success of programs effective in meeting the learning needs of adults.

Chapter Two

Graduate Degree Programs for Professional Adult Educators

Roy J. Ingham
Gardner Hanks

Graduate degree programs for the preparation and upgrading of adult educators were first established half a century ago. Since then the number of such programs has increased remarkably, though vigorous research to assess the relative effectiveness of such programs is lacking. In this chapter, we present an overview of the state of the art in graduate adult education and propose a new method for the design of graduate programs for professional adult educators.

Graduate degree programs in adult education were initiated in the 1930s, and the first doctorate in the field was awarded in 1935 by Columbia University. Since then, various aspects of the state of graduate studies in adult education have been investigated (see Ingham and Qazilbash, 1968; Ingham,

17

Munro, and Massey, 1970; Griffith and Cloutier, 1972; and Knox, 1973). Ingham and Robbins' (1977) survey of graduate programs in the United States and Canada serves as the basis for the present report.

Of the thirty-seven universities responding to the survey by Ingham and Robbins, all reported that they had a master's degree program, fifteen offered an educational specialist's degree, and twenty-six had a doctoral program. The specialist's degree, an intermediate degree between the master's and the doctorate, is relatively new; none of the respondents reported having had this degree program before 1960, and nine of the specialist's programs began in the 1970s.

Thirty-six respondents provided usable information on the backgrounds of their faculty members. These thirty-six programs had 101 full-time and 107 part-time faculty members. The means of 2.8 full-time and 2.9 part-time faculty members per program represent a substantial increase over the means of 1.6 full-time and 1.9 part-time reported by Griffith and Cloutier (1972). All but seven of the faculty members in the responding programs held the doctorate degree, and seventy-six full-time and sixty-three part-time faculty held doctorates in adult education.

In 1970-1971, the sixty-six departments that responded to Griffith and Cloutier's survey reported 1,697 master's degree students and 1,110 doctoral students. In 1976-1977, Ingham and Robbins found 2,171 master's degree students and 1,284 doctoral students in thirty-seven departments that answered their questionnaire. These figures seem to indicate a substantial increase in the number of graduate students in adult education during the early 1970s. A breakdown of the students reported to Ingham and Robbins shows 488 full-time and 1,683 part-time master's degree students and 616 full-time and 668 part-time doctoral students. Interestingly, although slightly over half (1,751) of the total 3,455 students reported were women, of the doctoral students, 646 were men and 638 were women. Most students were between the ages of twenty-five and fifty-four and most had been employed either in adult education or in another educational field before entering these graduate programs. However, four departments reported that at least half of their students came from fields outside of education.

Although decreasing financial resources have affected many university programs in recent years, adult education departments have fared remarkably well in terms of financial aid available to their students. Only five departments reported a substantial decrease in available funds, while three reported a moderate decrease. Four departments had enjoyed a substantial increase in financial assistance for their students, and eight stated that they had a moderate increase. Fourteen departments showed no change. However, the figures for financial support were not adjusted for inflation. Thus, for example, those departments reporting no change may have experienced a decline in real dollars due to inflation.

We thus see that graduate programs in adult education still seem to be expanding in terms of numbers of faculty members and students. Now we must examine graduate studies in adult education in qualitative terms. Perhaps the major responsibility of graduate programs in adult education is to increase the quality of practice in the field. Ideally, the holders of advanced degrees in adult education should be able to recognize unsatisfactory conditions within the programs in which they are employed, formulate reasonable desired states of affairs (goals) for each unsatisfactory condition, and systematically and humanely apply the knowledge created by the behavioral sciences to change an unsatisfactory condition to a desired one. To ascertain how well graduate programs are fulfilling this major responsibility, Ingham and Robbins asked the respondents in each graduate department to list important conditions within the field of adult education that were in need of improvement and to answer a series of questions about how they were preparing students to respond to those conditions.

Many of their respondents cited ineffective practices. Eighteen respondents either mentioned specific areas of practice (for example, needs assessment, teaching, program planning, evaluation) that were unsatisfactory or stated that practice in general needed improvement. Eleven respondents mentioned the failure to coordinate adult education programs with other agencies—both educational and noneducational—and five respondents indicated that they felt practitioners had insufficient community development skills.

In addition to their concern about ineffective practice, some respondents felt that adult education was a field that needed a greater degree of legitimization. Mention was made of the marginal nature of adult education programs and the failure of society to embrace the lifelong learning concept. Nine respondents pointed specifically to a failure on the part of the field to establish the concept that adult education practitioners must receive special training. As one respondent wrote, "[There is] a lack of awareness on the part of administrators, who hire, and practitioners, who perform in the field, that adult education training is needed to perform on the job."

Another area of concern to the respondents was research. Six respondents felt that more research was needed, while three indicated that the failure to utilize research findings in practice was of concern to their programs.

The response of the graduate schools to these unsatisfactory conditions was fairly predictable. Coursework was given as the response to concerns over ineffective practice. If program planning was thought to be poor, for example, then a course was offered in program planning. In a few instances, the surveyors suspected that some of the respondents deemed some areas of practice unsatisfactory simply to justify the existence of a particular course in their program. Concerns about legitimization were also addressed through courses, although other methods, such as faculty involvement with the community, were also mentioned. Improving the supervision of dissertations was one answer to concerns over research.

The survey also asked respondents to rate the contributions of their graduates to alleviating the unsatisfactory conditions in the field. In general, those responding to the survey felt that their graduates were making moderate to significant contributions. However, their conclusions were based largely on impressionistic feelings. Many respondents left blank the space for evidence to back their claims, and no respondent cited an objective study.

There is some irony in the conclusions that might be drawn from this survey. On the one hand, professors seem to be using the traditional coursework approach of arts and sciences graduate education as their response to the unsatisfactory conditions in the field. They seem to feel that this approach is moderately successful, even though their evidence for this claim is neither objective nor scientific. On the other hand, the respondents recognize that the field has failed to accept the notion that training is required to become an adequate adult education practitioner. After fifty years of graduate studies in adult education, it is still possible for persons with no university training in the field to assume positions of leadership.

The inability of the graduate programs in the field to clearly establish the superiority of the university-trained adult educator over the untrained one must be seen as a major failure of our graduate departments. We hypothesize that one reason for this failure has been the inability of many graduates to make effective use of the knowledge they have acquired in school. Dewey ([1929] 1960) once criticized education in general for a "devotion to training in technical and mechanical skills on the one hand and to laying in a store of abstract information on the other" rather than the "development of intelligence as a method of action" (p. 253). This criticism seems especially applicable to professional education.

Like other forms of professional education, programs for the preparation of adult educators have been overly influenced by the arts and sciences model of graduate education. The curricula of graduate adult education departments often stress the creation of knowledge or the teaching of specific practices rather than the methods by which knowledge can be used systematically and humanely to design plans of action for changing existing conditions into preferred conditions. In the rest of this chapter, we provide documentation to support this assertion and suggest a method by which improved plans of action can be designed. We also suggest curricular changes that will be needed to implement such a method in graduate departments of adult education.

Many authors have proposed curriculum changes in graduate education for adult educators (Boyd, 1969; Chamberlain, 1960; Dickerman, 1964; Douglah and Moss, 1969; Essert, 1960; Knowles, 1962; Liveright, 1964). The plan we present here is

22   Graduate Programs for Professional Adult Educators

not exclusively for adult educators but for all professional educators. Our approach is based on two principles. First, unlike any other approach, our approach is developed from criticism of the effectiveness of the work of professional adult educators. Because professions are by definition service-oriented, and adult education is considered to merit this classification (Liveright, 1964), ideas for professional education not explicitly grounded in the existing or potential effect on clients are deprived of their chief source of validity.

Second, our approach recognizes that professional educators need a general method or discipline that they can use to develop effective plans of action for their clients. Many evaluative studies of the professions and professional education in general claim that professionals are failing to satisfy basic social needs and that professional schools are in large part to blame (Argyris and Schön, 1974; Brooks, 1967; Gross and Osterman, 1972; Mayhew, 1971; Mayhew and Ford, 1974; Schein and Kommers, 1972). Most of these studies also include proposed reforms in professional education. The need for a general method which might be used by professionals in developing courses of action for meeting client needs is recognized by Simon (1969). Rather than the methods of science, as now formulated, he proposes that we need a "science of the artificial," or a science of *design,* the term he uses to refer to the functions of all professionals. Simon claims that "Everyone designs who devises courses of action aimed at changing existing situations into preferred ones. The intellectual activity that produces material artifacts is not different from the one that devises a new sale plan for a company or a social welfare policy for a state. Design so construed is the core of all professional training; it is the principal work that distinguishes the professions from the sciences" (p. 35).

At a more general level of analysis, some argue that the process of thinking about what actions should be taken to resolve problematic situations can be greatly improved through the use of systematic methods that provide a guide to reflective thought. Miller, Galanter, and Pribram (1960) note that "The advantages of having plans to generate plans is so great that no intelligent automaton, living or dead, could get along without them. . . they permit men to be creative in significant ways in a wide variety of situations" (pp. 178-179).

The general argument presented here is also neatly expressed by Jensen (1964), who maintains that adult education, like other professions, seeks to improve "some unsatisfactory state of affairs. . . of everyday life" (p. 106). The task, he claims, is to organize knowledge "in such a way as to give better practical control over factors associated with the problems which the adult education practitioner is facing" (p. 107).

On the basis of the foregoing arguments, one might claim confidently that a critical function of all professionals is to design and execute plans of action for improving the unsatisfactory situations of their clients. Effective plans for improving the present state of any particular situation can be designed if this process is guided by some general method. Thus the quality of professional practice in adult education would be improved considerably if professionals were to use a general method or, to use Simon's (1969) phrase, a "science of design," when creating plans of action. Given this position, our task is to identify the components of a method for designing particular plans of action.

One such method has been developed by one of the authors (Ingham, 1972). It is called a Method of Designing Action Systems (MODAS). Although its conceptualization draws heavily on the work of Simon (1969), MODAS includes a more detailed description of the procedures that one can use to design a plan. Formulations of other general methods that could be used to direct thinking about practice in particular professional fields have been developed by Mitchell (1973) and Yura and Walsh (1973) in nursing; Rosenstein (1968) and Asimow (1962) in engineering; Checkland (1975) in management science; Weed (1969) in medicine; Vinter (1967) in social work; and Lang and Burnette (1974) in architecture. Although these authors do not claim their methods are applicable to other professions, their approaches have points of similarity with MODAS. In addition, Nadler (1967) and Adelson (1972) have developed methods somewhat similar to MODAS, methods that they believe are applicable to various professions. The primary differences between their approaches and MODAS are that MODAS makes systematic use of the findings of social science research, information about the context in which the situation exists, and feedback from the implementation of the plan of action.

MODAS, as a formal system for designing plans of action, can be most efficiently used to change unsatisfactory conditions that have persisted for some time and have not responded to efforts to bring about a more desirable state of affairs. Clearly, less costly and less time-consuming techniques, such as asking the advice of experienced practitioners, should be tried before a decision is reached to use MODAS. Pirsig's (1975) observations on this point are relevant. He describes a complex, logical system like MODAS as an "enormous juggernaut, a huge bulldozer —slow, tedious, rumbling, laborious, but invincible. It takes twice as long, five times as long, maybe a dozen times as long as informal mechanic's technique, but you know in the end you're going to *get* it" (p. 100).

Professional practitioners, however, unlike motorcycle mechanics, frequently confront situations in which the desired state of affairs is indefinite and subject to change as clients redefine it as a consequence of movement relative to it. Thus, although we cannot with assurance claim that MODAS in the end will "get it," we feel justified in claiming that it is a method suited to the design of plans of action in adult education graduate programs. Further, several doctoral dissertations have used MODAS to design plans of action for various types of adult education agencies. (See Freed, 1977; Kuhling, 1977; Malone, 1973; McKendry, 1979; Newsom, 1976; Thompson, 1976.)

The Steps of MODAS

Our description of MODAS should provide sufficient information for professionals who desire to develop a curriculum incorporating a design method to do so. MODAS consists of twelve steps, each of which represents a capability to be developed. For each step of the method we specify its function, provide criteria for evaluating satisfactory performance of that step, and offer some suggestions for teaching that step. The prescriptions contained in the proposed curriculum rest on four assumptions. First, situations that are to be changed by professionals are so complex as to require a team of experts working cooperatively. One person will, in all likelihood, be incapable of designing and implementing effective plans of action. Second, the clients, the persons whose situations the practitioner is attempting to change, must be an integral part of the design team (Schein and Kommers, 1972; Stringer, 1972). Third, some of the knowledge required to formulate effective plans of action can be learned only through direct involvement with the situation to be regulated and its context (Argyris and Schön, 1974; Ruesch, 1975). Fourth, the knowledge now yielded by the social and behavioral sciences is not in a form compatible for use with design methods but can be developed into such a form. Although some writers, for example, Zetterberg (1962), seem to imply that social science findings are in a readily usable form, others do not agree (see Carter, 1968; National Science Foundation, 1969, p. 15).

Step 1. Describe the Present State of a Situation.

Function. The description of the present state will be compared with the desired state to enable the observer to determine if the present action system is sufficient.

Definition. A *situation* is a phenomenon that is a consequence of human actions; for example, "Teachers have left the agency at a rate of 25 percent per year for the past five years."

Criteria. The description must be reliable. It must be expressed in terms of sensory data and absolute, rather than relative, quantitative terms. It must specify the perspective and purpose of the observer.

Instruction. Practice in describing situations that occur in adult education agencies is perhaps the most effective experience for acquiring the ability to produce a description that meets the criteria. Often the sources of a description may be interviews with practitioners rather than direct observation. Under these conditions, reliability may be difficult to achieve and precise quantitative data are not usually attainable. An introductory exercise is considered the most appropriate activity for gathering and presenting descriptive data about the field, not only at the national level, such as reported by Johnstone and Rivera (1965) and by the National Center for Education Statistics (1972), but also within particular local agencies.

Methodological Issues. Procedures for arriving at a good description are difficult to specify. In spite of the apparent simplicity of this step, description evidently is not a strong suit of the social sciences. A tendency exists among those attempting to describe some discrete event or object to classify rather than describe, that is, to name the class of phenomena to which the discrete event or object observed belongs. For example, if an observer's attention is directed toward a discrete object and he or she is asked to describe the object, most observers name the class of phenomena to which the object belongs, such as "a cup" or "a pen," rather than identify the attributes of the object or offer sensory data. Clearly, in everyday conversation, naming facilitates communication. However, when applying formal design methods, one must provide a description of the observed phenomenon that allows persons not observing the phenomenon to decide independently if the classification (to be made in step 3) is a valid one. Useful discussions of this topic are offered by Larrabee (1964, pp. 93-124), Meehan (1968, pp. 32-46), Riker (1957), Toulmin and Baier (1952), Benne, Chin, and Bennis (1969), and Smith (1968).

Step 2. Describe the Desired State of the Situation.

Function. This description may express the desired state of the situation or the state of the situation that will be desired at some specified future time. Although this step and step 1 may be separated for analytical purposes, they occur concurrently in human behavior. Together, they make up one of the elements of the basic unit of human behavior proposed by Miller, Galanter, and Pribram (1960)—testing, the act of determining whether a present condition is congruent with some image of what that condition ought to be.

Definition. Using the example in step 1, the desired state of this situation might be "Teachers should leave the agency at a rate not greater than 10 percent in any given year, beginning next year."

Criteria. The description should meet the criteria in step 1, and it should include the time at which the desired state is to be realized.

Instruction. Following an introductory lecture and discussion on this topic, students may be asked to locate and critique desired states of situations found in the literature, particularly those articles describing programmatic efforts. *Lifelong Learning: The Adult Years,* published by the Adult Education Association of the United States, contains articles of this type. Practice in obtaining this information from others can also be gained in interviews with practitioners, as noted in step 1.

Methodological Issues. The major difficulty encountered in this step is to determine whose desired state is to be considered *the* desired state: the practitioner's? the client's? the organization's? the public's? some combination of these? Fortunately, the considerable literature on this subject, much of it under the rubric of needs assessment and goal analysis, provides some answers to these questions. Discussions of this topic are offered by Friedmann (1973), Gross (1964, pp. 486-537), and Mager (1972). A second issue is how one is to determine the desired quantitative state of the situation. This determination may be explicit or implicit in the policy of the organization. In the absence of such standards, persons involved in this task can often agree on whether they want more or less of a particular characteristic. To determine precisely how much usually requires considerable negotiation and skillful group leadership.

The reader may be wondering why the term *problem* has not been used in the discussion up to this point, since the examples used in steps 1 and 2 may look like problems. The reason is that *problem,* as commonly used, may refer to any of the following: the situation to be changed, the causes for this situation, or the desired states. Rather than using such an ambiguous term, we prefer more precise terms, such as those used here, even though they are not in keeping with the prevailing style.

We reserve the term *problem* to refer to a "lack of knowledge of means" (Newell and Simon, 1972, p. 72). Thus, if a practitioner does not know how to change a present situation to a desired one, a problem may be said to exist.

Step 3. Formulate a Rationale for the Desired State.

Function. The rationale will substantiate the value of the desired state.

Definition. A *rationale* is a set of underlying reasons. The rationale may be expressed as the answer to the question, Why is the desired state desirable?

Criteria. This statement should take into account the value systems of the client, the practitioner, the profession, the community, and the culture. It is assumed that the change from the present to the desired state will affect the level of satisfaction all persons identified (Pepper, 1958).

Instruction. Practice in acquiring answers from others to questions about rationale can be gained during interviews with practitioners. It is also important to examine one's own answers to this question. A discussion among students regarding the question, Why do I want to be an adult educator? is one procedure for developing their skills in value clarification and also for yielding important substantive information for each student.

Methodological Issues. With this step, one enters the realm of ethics. To ask the question, Why is the desired state desirable? and then ask, Why are those reasons appropriate? is to urge respondents to answer in terms of their conception of the good, the beautiful, or the true. In short, instrumental answers are soon exhausted, and the basic values that the respondents hold are evoked. (See Simon, 1959, chap. 3, for a discussion of this issue.) Because most people are reluctant to reveal this kind of information, the interviewer must exercise great skill and sensitivity and establish a relationship of trust. (See Rogers, 1968, chap. 11; Selltiz, Wrightsman, and Cook, 1976, chap. 9.)

Step 4. Classify the Observed Situation.

Function. The classification of the situation as an example of a concept is used to locate the relevant literature.

Definitions. To *classify* is to assign to a category; in this case, the category is to be a social science concept. For example, a test score may be classified as an instance of the concept of achievement. The concept used to classify the observed situation is referred to as the *purpose concept.*

Criteria. A good classification is one in which the attributes of the observed situation match those contained in the definition of the concept. Concepts that have been extensively researched are preferable to those that have not, assuming that the first criterion is met.

Instruction. Exercises in which three or four students classify observed situations are probably the best means for developing this skill. Written test cases provided by the instructor may be used initially, followed by cases taken from direct observation of situations in an adult education activity or from interviews with practitioners. To succeed, students must learn not to race for explanation before classifying the situation; that is, they must resist the urge to specify the solution strategy before they have attained a high level of confidence about the class of phenomena to be controlled. For example, many graduate students when asked to classify the observed situation of "a person enrolled in a course who attended a few classes but no longer attends" say that the problem is one of motivation, that this person does not attend because he is not motivated. In responding this way, students are jumping to a conclusion before searching for the concept that fits this situation. Useful concepts include *dropout* and *attrition.* See Dewey (1929), Wilson (1963), Fraenkel (1973), and Benne, Chin, and Bennis (1969) for discussions of the importance of classification.

Methodological Issues. Most design and problem-solving methods neglect this crucial step. Without it, the location of the relevant knowledge and literature is difficult. By way of speculation, ineffective plans of action are often the consequence of the designer's choice of the wrong purpose concept; or, in medical terminology, an incorrect diagnosis leads to ineffective treatment. A serious methodological issue that arises in efforts to classify is that definitions in the social sciences do not contain terms that describe observable attributes of the phenomena of interest.

There exists a considerable debate over how to operationalize social science concepts (Broadbeck, 1963, pp. 48-55; Blumer, 1940; Blalock and Blalock, 1968, pp. 7-14). It is our position, following Broadbeck, that an effort should be made to use those terms in the definition that represent observable phenomena. Even though technical dictionaries for the various disciplines contain definitions that do not meet the criteria for this step, they are almost always more useful than general dictionaries.

Step 5. Locate Explanatory Systems.

Function. Explanatory systems provide general rules upon which to construct a plan of action. An explanatory system for the chosen purpose concept hypothesizes about how the class of phenomena represented by the concept can be controlled.

Definitions. An *explanatory system* consists of a set of entities and a set of rules specifying the relationship among those entities. In social science research, these entities are called *independent variables*; in design methodology, they are called *means concepts*.

Criteria. A satisfactory explanatory system must be relevant to the class of phenomena to be controlled and must constitute reliable knowledge. An explanatory system is relevant if the definition of the purpose concept selected in step 4 is identical to that of the purpose concept contained in the explanatory system. Notice that the definitions, not merely the terms, must match. For example, the purpose concept *withdrawal* is the subject of many explanatory systems; in locating an explanatory system relevant to one's own purpose concept, one must compare the definitions of the terms used. The means concept must be translated into concrete referents that have low levels of ambiguity; a concrete referent is an observable instance of the concept. If more than one explanatory system is found for a given purpose concept, the one with the highest reliability should be used. Reliability—a high level of confidence in the claims made by the explanatory system—can be determined by the procedure recommended by Zetterberg (1965).

Instruction. Instruction to develop skill in locating relevant and reliable explanatory systems should proceed in two ways. First, students should take courses in the social sciences to learn the concepts and explanatory systems related to the phenomena that they as practitioners will attempt to regulate. Second, after the coursework, students should be given the opportunity to locate explanatory systems with which they may be unfamiliar and which are relevant to a class of phenomena that they have identified for a particular situation. This independent work will help students develop skills in learning how to learn about an unfamiliar subject and in independently determining relevance and reliability.

Methodological Issues. A major methodological issue that arises in assessing explanatory systems is that no explanation is complete; that is, none contains all variables that are *sufficient* to specify the final entailment of the system (see Meehan, 1968). Social scientists have made little effort to aggregate the existing bits and pieces of knowledge into explanatory systems (National Science Foundation, 1969, p. 15). One approach to this task is Dynamo, a programming language that can be used to build explanatory systems with soft data (Bossel, 1974). Bossel's approach is to "(1) collect a large set of verbal statements and intuitive concepts about partial aspects of the problem (that is, about the 'real system'); (2) to tie these statements and concepts together in a consistent manner; (3) to translate the resulting 'image system' ('model') of verbal statements and graphs into a computer program; (4) to let this computer program 'simulate' the time-path of the 'real system' by operating on the 'image system'; starting with given initial conditions" (p. 24). Another method of accomplishing this task is demonstrated by Simon (1957).

Explanatory systems may be produced by procedures other than those called scientific or even rational. Human actions, as Jantsch (1975) claims, are much too complex to be guided solely by the closed systems of science. Explanations must also use information produced by the "perception of patterns, the understanding of connotations, and the intuitive and analogical appreciation of events" (Ruesch, 1975, p. 294).

Boulding (1956, p. 16) provides further elaboration of this point and a more general discussion of how we form our knowledge of the world. Hudson and others (1976, pp. 19-22) offer additional insight into this topic.

Step 6. Design an Initial Plan of Action by Translating the Abstract Means Concepts into Their Concrete Referents.

Function. This plan specifies those actions that the practitioner might take to regulate the class of phenomena represented by the purpose concept. For example, if the purpose concept is labor turnover, one of the means concepts in a relevant explanatory system may be rewards. Three ways to operationalize this concept are: "(1) increase the number of different types of rewards; (2) increase the employee's choice of which types of rewards he can obtain; (3) increase the validity of the employee's expectations of obtaining rewards through communications about the reward system" (Porter and Speers, 1973, p. 172).

The means concept is used in this step to generate plans that address the class of concepts of which the particular observed situation is a member. In later steps, this plan will be refined to address the particular observed situation.

Definition. Means concept, as noted in step 5, is synonymous with independent variable.

Criteria. The attributes of the concrete referents must match those contained in the definition of the respective means concepts. Gaining consensus by two or more experts is one way to attain greater confidence in the choice of concrete referents of various means concepts.

Instruction. Development of this skill can take place in the courses suggested in step 5. Students should be given practice in translating concepts with which they are familiar, as well as unfamiliar concepts presented in class, and those identified as a result of interviews with practitioners recommended in step 4. Practice can also be gained by presenting students with a concept and several descriptions of actions a practitioner might take. Students are then asked to choose which action most logically follows given a particular definition of that concept. Here, as with explanatory systems, translating unfamiliar concepts teaches students how to apply appropriate criteria to the choice of concrete referents as well as providing substantive information.

Methodological Issues. Unless definitions of the means concepts identifying their attributes are available, a high level of uncertainty will prevail in the identification of the concrete referents of those concepts. This condition is the reverse of the one present in step 4. If the source of an explanatory system is a research article, the process used to measure the independent variable provides an operational definition of the means concept. Often, however, the definition of the means concept does not supply concrete referents; sometimes no definition is provided. If one is uncertain of the researcher's definition of a concept, one should try to locate another explanatory system. Although one may find a definition in a technical dictionary, one cannot be certain that this is the same definition that the researcher had in mind. In some cases, one simply cannot find a relevant explanatory system for a given purpose concept.

Step 7. Identify and Measure Exogenous Variables Related to the Purpose Concept and Refine the Initial Plan of Action.

Function. The specification of exogenous variables provides a basis for modifying the initial plan of action.

Definition. Exogenous variables in an explanatory system are those variables that affect the purpose concept but cannot be controlled by the designer of the plan (Churchman, 1968; Simon, 1969). For example, in studying educational achievement, Dave (1963) identifies variables that measure the quality of living in the student's home and reports that these have high positive correlations with school achievement. Such exogenous variables must be taken into account by teachers designing plans of instruction. Although teachers have no way to control these variables, they must make modifications in their plans to address exogenous variables that affect achievement.

Criteria. Exogenous variables that are part of explanatory systems that have been judged reliable through established verification procedures are preferable to those that have not met this test. Exogenous variables that have been identified by expert practitioners are also considered reliable.

Step 8. Prepare a Method for the Process and Product Evaluation of the Plan Prior to its Implementation.

Function. Information obtained from the process evaluation of the plan will enable refinements to be made during the plan's implementation. The product evaluation provides information for judging if the plan has effected the desired state specified in step 2.

Definitions. Process evaluation "provides periodic feedback to persons responsible for implementing plans and procedures. It has three objectives: (1) to detect or predict defects in the procedural design or its implementation during the implementation stages; (2) to provide information for programmed decisions; and (3) to maintain a record of the procedure as it occurs" (Stufflebeam, 1971, p. 354). Product evaluation "assesses the extent to which ends are being attained with respect to change efforts within the system" (Stufflebeam, 1971, p. 354).

Criteria. The process of developing an evaluation plan is complex, and the criteria are too numerous to list here. All texts on evaluation offer criteria. Approaches to evaluation most consistent with design methods are offered by Provus (1971), Stake (1967), and Stufflebeam (1971).

Instruction. Instruction in evaluation should include at least six semester hours of coursework, or the equivalent. Whereas a traditional curriculum emphasizes research courses, a curriculum for designers should emphasize the application of design knowledge during a field experience. The use of the total design method is considered essential to the development of competence in this step.

Methodological Issues. Evaluation provides the third major source of information in this design method, the other two being the explanatory system and the measurements of exogenous variables, or contextual knowledge. Evaluative information enables the practitioner to make refinements based on actual operating conditions. Students must learn to thoroughly evaluate plans of action, and practioners' methodology should include an evaluative component.

Step 9. Implement the Plan of Action.

Function. The implementation of the plan will, presumably, produce the desired state of affairs.

Definition. An *action* is a human behavior.

Criteria. For an action to be performed well, it must be conducted with skill. (See Bromley, 1966, pp. 49-61, for a comprehensive analysis of skilled behavior.)

Methodological Issues. The verbal statements in the plan cannot be directly translated into actions, although they can identify those features that one must observe if actions are to be effective. So, as Grattan observes, there may always be a gap between the idea and the practice (1971, p. 303). How a plan is executed is, of course, critical. Even an excellent plan, a composition by Mozart, for example, will not achieve the desired results if performed poorly. Numerous factors can impede skillful performance; for a discussion of these see Ruesch (1975, pp. 293-309) and Mager and Pipe (1970). Expertise in executing a plan is best acquired through observing a skilled and polished performer and then by having a skilled observer criticize one's own actions. Thus, field experience of some form is essential. Argyris and Schön (1974) present an excellent description of how to conduct effective field experiences for professional education.

Step 10. Implement the Process Evaluation Plan.

Function. By implementing the process evaluation plan, one obtains information that will enable one to improve, through modification, the plan of action (Ruesch, 1975, pp. 294-296). Successive implementations of modified plans of action should similarly be subject to process evaluation.

Criteria. Same criteria as those for step 9. (Also, see Ruesch, 1975.)

Instruction. Same as step 9.

Methodological Issues. Evaluation is essentially a process of making judgments about the degree of congruity between a desired state of some entity (a standard) and the observed existing state of that entity. Thus, the chief concerns are with reliability and validity of the observed information and the setting of standards. The relevant methodological issues are treated at length in the references cited for steps 1, 2, and 8.

The process of evaluation in itself does not provide information that can be used directly to guide action. Evaluative information is the basis for inferences about what changes should be made. The information that guides action may be called *functional information,* knowledge that can be used to effect change.

Step 11. Modify the Plan of Action if Necessary.

Function. To redirect action toward the desired state. In practice, modifications may occur immediately or as an integral part of step 10; however, different analytical procedures are required for gathering data (step 10) and using it (step 11).

Criteria. A good modification will reduce serious adverse consequences resulting from the implementation of the plan and will, when implemented, produce satisfactory movement toward the desired state. Such progress will be evidenced by intermediate product evaluations.

Instruction. Experience with the total process of implementing, monitoring, and modifying a plan under the direction of a skillful practitioner is necessary to develop competence in this step. If a favorable disposition toward this task is not present, students may acquire it by precept from those with whom they identify as role models, ideally the practitioners whom they encounter during field experience and their faculty advisors.

Methodological Issues. Because one comes to like the plans that one has created, it is difficult to accept the need for change. Thus, the methodological issue here is more human than technical. Perhaps the most productive attitude to develop is a healthy and honest curiosity about the results of one's plans. Dewey ([1929] 1960) reminds us how complex the planning process is when he states that "Judging, planning, choice, no matter how thoroughly conducted, and action no matter how prudently executed, never are the sole determinants of any outcome. Alien and indifferent natural forces, unforeseeable conditions enter in and have a decisive voice" (p. 7).

Step 12. Conduct the Final Product Evaluation.

Function. The final product evaluation is conducted at the time specified in step 2 to determine if the present state of affairs is congruent with the desired state.

Criteria. Same criteria as for step 8.

Instruction. See step 8.

Methodological Issues. If the present state of affairs and the desired state are congruent, one may conclude that the present plan of action is sufficient and may be used again with confidence whenever analogous new situations are encountered by practitioners. If the present state and the desired state are noncongruent, examination of all steps of the method to locate the error is necessary. As a general rule of thumb, large degrees of incongruity are usually the result of errors made during the first five steps.

Conclusion

Anyone attempting to change his department's professional education curriculum to one that reflects a design philosophy had best prepare to meet formidable resistance. Such an effort will be perceived by most faculty, within both arts and science schools and professional schools, not merely as a substitution of one set of courses for another, but as a bold theoretical change. For it is the case that a fundamental difference exists between the methodology and postulates of the domains of science and those of the professions; or, similarly, between science and technology (Fores, 1971); or, in more elemental terms, between knowledge and action (Argyris and Schön, 1974; Cassidy, 1960; Dewey, [1929] 1960). Scientists seek to discover necessary, or causal, relationships between classes of phenomena without preconceptions of what those relationships ought to be. In contrast, professionals design action systems that are sufficient to serve human purposes in particular situations.

Professional educators who want to bring about major curriculum change in professional education may find the strategies proposed by Argyris and Schön (1974) and Schein and Kommers (1972) to be of some value. However, to close on a disquieting note, the latter authors warn that "there is little incentive in today's professional school to 'rock the boat.' The system is thoroughly bureaucratized and basically comfortable for both faculty and students. Unless a professor has strong motivation to innovate, he will not have the emotional energy to go through the change process required to convert to a new system and then to keep the new system going in the face of regressive forces" (p. 143). We believe, however, that the potential benefits to the client justify accepting the challenge.

Chapter Three

Training Part-Time Instructional Staff

Donald W. Mocker
Elizabeth Noble

Our discussion of part-time adult teachers refers to those teachers whose employment situations are characterized by the following: (1) the work week is shorter than thirty-five hours and the term of employment is nine months a year or shorter; (2) the wages are determined by an hourly pay rate that does not include fringe benefits such as hospitalization, vacation, or sick leave; or (3) the employee is considered a substitute employee and thus does not receive the employment benefits granted regular employees. (This status may at times include persons working forty or more hours per week.)

The training of part-time teachers and the training of full-time teachers should be differentiated because each group plays a different role in the educational process and consequently requires different skills. Part-time teachers are primarily experts in subject matter and usually have little responsibility for the educational process other than the course or courses that they are teaching. Full-time teachers or supervisors, in contrast, are often responsible for the total planning process, which includes integrating courses, needs assessment, curriculum development, long-range planning, and recruitment. These processes require specialized skills.

Prior to 1965, few researchers or methodologists wrote about the selection of curriculum for the training of either part-time or full-time adult education teachers. Those who did study training were primarily concerned with graduate-level programs and not the training of classroom personnel. Relevant literature includes Houle's (1956) description of levels of leadership in adult education ("the pyramid of leadership"); the Commission of Professors of Adult Education (1964) and Liveright (1964, 1968) addressed the issue of the objectives of graduate programs. Veri (1970) identified four models used to develop graduate programs.

Studying the more specific topic of classroom teacher competencies, Marshall and Copley (1967) developed a hierarchy of thirty-three problems that confront adult basic education (ABE) teachers, Knowles (1970) identified six criteria that should govern the selection of general adult education teachers, and Bruny (1970) ranked twenty-two needs of general adult educators. Davison (1970) described the qualifications and socioeconomic characteristics of ABE instructors in British Columbia. Niemi and Davison (1971) developed a model to analyze ABE teacher training in order to guide the selection and training of ABE teachers. Fenn's (1972) research identified the kinds of knowledge, skills, and attitudes needed by ABE teachers to achieve minimum effectiveness. In a similar study, Smith (1972) conducted research to determine the perceptions of the competencies needed by ABE teachers. Mocker (1974) identified, classified, and ranked 173 distinct kinds of knowledge, behaviors, and attitudes appropriate for ABE teachers. James (1976) clustered Mocker's inventory of competency statements into related groupings and identified the utility of the competency clusters as they were perceived by professors of adult education, ABE administrators, and ABE teachers.

A review of the literature shows that studies of teacher competencies tend to be descriptive. The lack of empirical research is noteworthy and indicates that the available data should be interpreted with caution.

Differentiated Training

Part-time employment has traditionally been very much a part of the adult education movement because it enhances the ability of administrators to meet the diverse needs of their target populations. Meeting these diverse needs of adults in an ever-changing social context has been achieved through a relatively informal educational stucture that allows flexibility. The ability to manage part-time personnel is a primary skill of the adult education administrator, for to maintain a program's flexibility and informal structure requires fluid planning, implementation, and evaluation. Because the subject matter competencies required by a program depend on learners' interest and enrollment, an adult education program's staffing cannot be based solely on institutional preferences. This need to change programs to serve the changing interests of adult learners is one of the central characteristics that differentiates adult education from other forms of education.

Most adult education programs thus depend on a cadre of part-time adult education teachers. Characteristically, these teachers are diverse, mobile, and responsive; they have the appropriate subject matter expertise, but many do not have training in the educational techniques specific to adult populations. By virtue of their background, they have not acquired the instructional competencies needed to provide the highest-quality educational experiences for adult learners. Most professional adult educators have long awaited a time when all adult education would be in the firm and stable hands of extensively trained, full-time teachers. Contrary to this pervasive view, the position taken here is that adult education administrators can continue to meet highly complex social and technological changes only by retaining a cadre of part-time teachers. The question is how to maintain a part-time instructional staff that is competent in the techniques of teaching adults.

Part-time instructional staff are likely to be used in larger numbers in the future, even though they lack specific preparation in adult education, because of the importance of economic factors. Economists call part-time employees secondary workers to indicate that their status regarding salary, fringe benefits, and security of employment is different from that of full-time employees. Community colleges, for example, find that they can employ three half-time persons for the cost of one full-time person (Bender and Bender, 1973). Declining enrollments and revenues lead to economic pressures which make it necessary for educational institutions to increase the proportion of part-time teachers to reduce the costs of instruction.

Employing part-time staff almost invariably produces a cadre of instructors who have not invested in their own professional preparation as adult educators. Those who must be prepared on an in-service basis for adult teaching require special programs that might not be necessary if the institution could afford to employ full-time professionally prepared adult educators. Hiring full-time teachers with training in adult education clearly presents a different set of problems from those encountered when part-time teachers are used.

What then is gained by attempting to solve the problem of staff development by employing full-time staff? There is greater control; however, the flexibility and diversity are lost, and this loss is significant in the long term. Employing full-time personnel seldom increases the ability of an organization to meet diverse needs in periods of social and technological change. Adult education is not a single activity with a single purpose; it is a locus of activities involving individuals for multiple purposes. Programs that rely on a cadre of full-time teachers may be appreciably less able to meet the needs of their clientele. A set organizational structure would be unlikely to accommodate the highly individualized learning needs of adults. A movement toward employing more full-time teachers would require major changes in organizational structure. Full-time staffs require a rigid and permanent structure while part-time staffs function best with a fluid and flexible structure, and such fluidity and flexibility are especially appropriate for serving the changing learning needs of an adult clientele.

The Cooperative Extension Service is unique among adult education programs in that it understands how a bureaucratic structure can undermine organizational flexibility. This program, the largest of all adult education programs, responds to learner needs by delegating the responsibility for program planning to local volunteer committees and having full-time professionals respond to local leadership.

Use of part-time staff thus appears a major asset to the field of adult education. It is also a factor in maintaining the noninstitutional character of adult education, which has permitted the field to expand without the bureaucratic restrictions common to other areas of education. For example, in colleges and universities several years may pass between the time a new degree program is proposed and the time it is implemented. In contrast, many adult education organizations, such as Cooperative Extension, can implement programs almost simultaneously with their development. Similarly, academic degree programs emphasize long-range goals, while adult education emphasizes short-term responsiveness to present needs. Therefore, the employment criterion that has tended to dominate in adult education is subject matter expertise, a response to the short-range goals of the learner.

The part-time staff of secondary workers is typically composed of persons who have full-time employment in their subject matter field and individuals working part-time to supplement their household's income. Although these teachers are usually not interested in becoming full-time educators, they often request in-service instruction in education techniques and methodologies (Harris and Parsons, 1975). Some of the cost savings from the employment of part-time staff could be invested in in-service training to create greater efficiency in programming efforts. This approach is one suggested in education competency studies and is currently being used by industry in training programs. Business and industry recognize that efficiency in instruction occurs when instructors with extensive practical experience are used to systematically train new and inexperienced personnel. However, subject matter experts often are not equipped to provide adequate and efficient instruction. Therefore, subject matter experts should be trained in techniques of adult instruction, group processing, testing, and teaching methodologies.

Part-time instructors in industry and general adult educators do not have the time or commitment to become competent in the philosophy of adult education or curriculum development. Their primary responsibility is to maintain competency in a subject area. These instructors are not removed from their jobs but engage in the education activities on a part-time basis (Miller, 1973-1974). Thus, training in the philosophy of adult education and principles of curriculum development should be available primarily to full-time trainers, administrators, and supervisors. By training managerial personnel in the philosophy of adult education and curriculum development and by having experts in a given subject matter teach their particular subject, industry has been able to rival educational programs outside the business community. Colleges and universities are becoming increasingly involved in community education, and they, too, will need diverse teaching resources to respond to rapidly changing adult learning interests.

Competencies of Part-Time Personnel

The following list of suggested competencies is a result of studies conducted at the Center for Resource Development in Adult Education, University of Missouri–Kansas City. A list of 605 competency statements was compiled from sixty-one documents selected from the literature and from unpublished reports written by university training staffs who conduct preservice institutes for ABE teachers. These statements were subsequently reduced to 173 statements. A selected group of adult educators from across the United States were impaneled to rank order the statements. The original set of 173 competency statements has been used with over 700 adult education teachers and program administrators. All studies were combined to produce one rank-ordered list, and the top twenty-four competencies were selected as those which should be used to train part-time adult education teachers. The top twenty-four competencies were selected because they seem to form a reasonable set of goals for a staff development effort and because they are competencies common to all adult education teachers. That is, none of the competencies in this list is particular to adult basic education, vocational education, or any other specialized group of adult education teachers.

A part-time adult education teacher should be able to:

1. communicate effectively with learners
2. develop effective working relationships with learners
3. reinforce positive attitudes toward learners
4. develop a climate that will encourage learners to participate
5. establish a basis for mutual respect with learners
6. adjust rate of instruction to the learners' rate of progress
7. adjust teaching to accommodate individual and group characteristics
8. differentiate between teaching children and teaching adults
9. devise instructional strategies that will develop the learners' confidence
10. maintain the learners' interest in classroom activities
11. adjust a program to respond to the changing needs of learners
12. use classrooms and other settings that provide a comfortable learning environment
13. recognize learners' potentiality for growth
14. place learners at their instructional level
15. summarize and review the main points of a lesson or demonstration
16. participate in a self-evaluation of teaching effectiveness
17. provide continuous feedback to the learners on their educational progress
18. select those components of a subject area that are essential to learners
19. coordinate and supervise classroom activities

20. determine those principles of learning that apply to adults
21. demonstrate belief in innovation and experimentation by willingness to try new approaches in the classroom
22. plan independent study with learners
23. apply knowledge of material and procedures gained from other teachers
24. relate classroom activities to the experience of learners

This list of competencies should not be interpreted as more than a general direction for staff development of part-time teachers. To use these competencies as absolute criteria or to infer too much from specific ranking detracts from the usefulness of the list. Of the twenty-four competencies, eighteen are instructional in nature. Of the remaining six, one is related to curriculum, two to scope and goal of adult education, and three to the learner. Thus part-time teachers do not need training in the area of curriculum development or in the history and philosophy of adult education. Curricular decisions will need to be made for the part-time teacher, leaving adult education history and philosophy to be studied by professors and full-time personnel. Staff development of part-time teachers should concentrate on the classroom and the interaction between the teacher and the learner. Competency in subject matter is assumed and little effort should be devoted to staff training in this area.

This list also suggests that emphasis must be placed on effective communication, effective working relationships with learners, and the creation of a positive learning climate in the classroom. Another implication drawn from this list is that staff development for part-time teachers is essential in the area of individualizing and adjusting instruction to meet learners' needs.

Summary

The employment of a staff of full-time teachers can be viewed as a replication of the public school model. An adult education curriculum is not based on the developmental process of teaching basic skills to children but rather on the episodic learning patterns of adults. Adult learning is problem-oriented and demands a teacher whose knowledge is current in a particular field.

The phenomenon of part-time staffing in adult education is to be valued and nurtured. It is not a second-rate system that originated by administrative fiat to save money but is a necessary part of the field to ensure its continued flexibility. The importance of part-time teachers should be recognized, and effective training programs should be developed to offer selective training that builds on part-time teachers' acknowledged fundamental base of expertise.

Chapter Four

Training Paraprofessional Instructors of Adults

Bettie Lee Yerka

The emergence of the paraprofessional concept in human service programs and its effect on employing agencies, on the paraprofessionals themselves, and on the consumers of human services have been acclaimed during the past two decades. The concept became widely popular during the 1960s and continued to develop through the 1970s. Many kinds of social legislation regarding vocational education, rehabilitation, health services, juvenile delinquency, senior citizens, and other programs include references to paraprofessionals. Pearl (1977, p. 232) predicts that "in the future the paraprofessional will work with all age groups; the greatest number . . . with adults, and adult education will become the largest and most important segment of educational activity."

Important statements of national policy and legislative proposals designate the creation of new paraprofessional careers as a major element of both antipoverty programs and national employment policy. Such statements testify to "the mood . . . to innovate and experiment with new methods of training and teaching, of manpower utilization and of organization and development in our social and economic relations" (Nixon, 1969, p. 204). Various results for these programs and for the groups affected have been envisioned by policy makers, administrators, legislators, program planners, trainers, supervisors, staff development personnel, and paraprofessionals themselves.

Many of these programs to train paraprofessionals have helped employees to discover meaningful work and have assisted social and educational agencies to achieve their goals by making available a supply of capable community workers. For instance, local paraprofessional workers can often establish rapport with members of a low-income community because they understand the life-style of neighborhood families. This rapport enables local paraprofessionals to act as links between an agency, the professional staff, and the clientele in the delivery of an agency's programs and services.

Providing Human Services

A major issue relative to paraprofessionalism is the meaning of providing service. Wright and Burmeister (1973) indicate that human services are organized cooperative responses to human needs. Many of people's needs are no longer met by one individual responding to another; rather, they are met through the development of agencies and programs whose trained staffs recognize and respond to the needs of specific groups of individuals. This complex human service network possesses both specializations and organizational forms of responding to human needs. "The way in which a human service operates depends . . . upon the definitions it accepts . . . assumptions about the nature of human problems determining the strategies adopted by human services for solution" (Wright and Burmeister, 1973, p. 17). Within this network, each organization makes decisions about the staffing style most useful to accomplishing its goals. For example, a study of paraprofessional status in 667 New York State school districts identified over 100 *types* of paraprofessionals in 94 percent of the districts (New York State Education Department, 1969).

Some rapidly growing human service programs have faced personnel shortages. Widespread, loosely coordinated efforts to alleviate these shortages have proliferated through community and junior colleges, technical institutes, professional schools, vocational centers, hospitals, professional organizations, and government agencies. Although the present political climate is more conservative than in the 1960s, new paraprofessionals continue to influence human service systems and are influenced by them. There is a vast literature on the ways paraprofessionals contribute to the improvement of human service practice—by reaching hitherto unreached people, providing new kinds of services, and introducing a new community ethos to agencies that have limited ties to communities.

In schools and all other human services, the individual in need of help (the consumer, client, or student) confronts organizational and positional structures. The actual helping, however, is performed through the combined efforts of many human service workers, each of whom has a set of duties and responsibilities that contribute to the organization's response to its clientele's needs. These duties, as Wright and Burmeister (1973) illustrate, include maintenance, service, outreach, evaluation, and others required to keep the organization healthy and able to carry out the goals and objectives for which it was formed.

The development of employees' potential—creating entry-level positions and devising meaningful promotion opportunities—is inherent in the concept of better utilization of human resources. A career lattice, for example, utilizes interrelationships among jobs to create promotional opportunities and facilitate mobility of workers among jobs. It provides for horizontal mobility to jobs at the same relative level of complexity in a different area of work, vertical mobility to more complex jobs in the same area of work, and diagonal mobility to more complex jobs in a different but related area of work. Difficulties in training programs for new paraprofessionals include agencies' inability or reluctance to develop career ladders and higher education's reluctance to institute necessary changes (although colleges with curricula for human services workers have granted degrees to paraprofessionals).

The paraprofessional, a person working under the direction of the professional in providing services directly to clients, either does not have professional credentials or does not wish to assume the role of a professional (Wright and Burmeister, 1973). Paraprofessionals who have less than the required or expected levels of professional training perform duties usually handled by the professional under the direct supervision of a certified person. As such, paraprofessionals are paid to assist a professional and may work in an institution, school, or service agency on tasks usually, but not always, performed by a professional (U.S. Department of Agriculture, Extension Service, 1973).

Paraprofesionals, however, are not always greeted with enthusiasm by professionals. The study of paraprofessionals in New York State School districts concluded that "the notion of a person in the school who is not a teacher, but who carries on some of the functions of a teacher—is not easily accepted by the hierarchy from teacher to state education chief. This is a movement that arose from expediency, without much planning or systematic effort to build support of the professional staff, without clear identification of their role and responsibility, and without involvement of the community or paraprofessionals themselves" (New York State Education Department, 1969, p. 1).

Thus the professionals' existence, role, and function in a given agency are critical to the development of paraprofessional services. In discussing the hallmarks of professionalism, Freidson (1970) refers to autonomy, the control of the content, if not the terms, of work; that is, professionals are self-directing in their work. A self-directing occupational group is likely to control the production and, in particular, the application of knowledge and skill to the work it performs. Also, a code of ethics or some other statement of good intentions represents a formal method of declaring that the occupation can be trusted and may be used to persuade society to grant the special status of autonomy.

What of the other occupational groups working in the organization dominated by professionals? Professionals are often said to be committed to and identified with their work so that its meaning for them is a central life interest. Paraprofessional workers may be more like industrial workers, subordinate not only to the authority of a bureaucratic office but also to the knowledge and judgment of professional experts. Some researchers characterize this authority as a kind of stratification; others, as a function of status: "The definition of the work—that is, how the client should behave and what other workers should do—is a partial expression of the hierarchy created by the office, and of the ideology stemming from the perspective of the office as well as of the purely technical character of the work itself" (Freidson, 1970, p. 90).

Characteristics and Utilization of Paraprofessionals

Compared with professionals, paraprofessionals are a mixed group: those with no training but with a willingness to enter into a helping role with the socially distressed; the poor who see in services the possibility of jobs and perhaps even careers; the partially trained (those with apprentice-like experience); and the militants who feel that the professions have wrongly excluded them from certain functions for which they are or could be certified (Grosser, Henry, and Kelly, 1969).

Hardcastle (1971) summarizes five major premises about the use of paraprofessionals in human services: providing new employment opportunities for low-income persons; alleviating the shortage of professional personnel; reducing staff costs in agencies; responding to environmental pressures (political, social, or economic); and improving the delivery and quality of services. Gartner and Riessman (1974) claim paraprofessionals generally retain a complicated mixture of their own past and their community ties, although they have become workers and this role defines many of their individual goals. Further, they become socialized by the agencies, professionals, institutions, and colleges with which they are associated and by the training they receive. They are a blend of the old and new.

In 1970, a two-year community college and a four-year college in upstate New York contracted to develop, implement, and evaluate a two-year training program for paraprofessionals employed in human services in a two-county area (Wright, n.d.). Results indicated no dominant pattern of paraprofessional utilization in agencies surveyed, although three basic patterns of deployment were evident. In general, the first pattern is one in which a professional and a paraprofessional work as a dyad, and the function of the paraprofessional is to assist the professional in performing professional tasks. The investigation did not uncover a clear differentiation of task assignments; as paraprofessionals learned by observation and experience, they performed more of the professionals' tasks.

The second pattern is one in which one professional coordinates and supervises the work of a number of paraprofessionals. In general, these paraprofessionals are assigned tasks to be performed in a relatively autonomous manner. This situation is frequently associated with the development of new services and new jobs. The professionals are often not as directly involved in the delivery of the same services as the paraprofessionals; rather, professionals provide support for the paraprofessionals' work and link it to other facets of the organization. This pattern may be found in organizations that have one professional who works with a number of paraprofessionals, each of whom has a different set of responsibilities in relation to the professional or all of whom have similar responsibilities.

In the third pattern, one paraprofessional is responsible to a number of professionals and generally functions as an aide to the professionals, while less frequently providing direct services to clients. Tasks assigned to the paraprofessional in this case are frequently those requiring less discretion, less education, and fewer skills than those required in the other two patterns.

Some agencies in this study used different staffing patterns for different paraprofessional functions. The investigators found no evidence that most of the organizations in the survey

had a clearly conceived idea, when they first employed paraprofessionals, about the functions the latter were to fulfill. The investigators caution that staffing patterns and functions evolve,
often independently, and may not represent what practitioners,
administrators, or paraprofessionals themselves would consider
ideal. This diversity of models is also evident in the wide assort-
ment of job-related evaluative criteria specified by administrators.

Wright and Burmeister (1973) suggest a hierarchy of four
paraprofessional utilization patterns. The nonprofessional has
low-level skills and knowledge, such as a library aide. The auxiliary performs tasks requiring more limited discretion and technical expertise than the professional, although much of the work
may be shared by the two, such as by a team of a teacher and a
classroom aide. The preprofessional is engaged in a supervised
internship in a program of professional higher education that is
developed by a college and a practicing cooperating agency and
specifies professional competencies. The new professional performs tasks not traditionally carried out by the professional;
tasks are nonroutine and perhaps only loosely supervised by the
professional, but the tasks require skills, experience with clientele, and information about the clientele and their needs. The
characteristics of each utilization pattern imply the nature of
training appropriate to achieve the agency's desired goals. The
roles and functions of professionals and paraprofessionals, their
relationships, and the training programs are directly interrelated
to the effectiveness of the business they are engaged in—bring-
ing needed services to clientele.

Development of Training

Program planners and personnel experts are concerned
with the acquisition of knowledge and skills by paraprofessionals. Some studies of training and performance in industry conclude that an assessment of the trainee's attitudes and skills
constitutes the best predictor of work success. Ultimately, however, most paraprofessional training programs are justified in
terms of how well the organization performs its functions, that
is, how program recipients are affected.

Little research has been published about paraprofessional training programs. Training, as a planned and organized process that develops a person's ability to perform a function in order to achieve a goal, is considered here as synonymous with education. Both are processes in which learning experiences are planned to develop specific knowledge, skills, and attitudes in the learner. The concept of paraprofessional work as a career emphasizes the development of paraprofessional jobs that offer in-service training, upgrading, and additional formal education. The body of literature mentioned earlier was accumulated as agencies and institutions increased their employment of paraprofessionals and as colleges and universities became involved in programming.

Many journal articles and books on paraprofessional programs describe specific activities in selected programs, especially their training content. Specifics of training efforts, such as trainees' remuneration, duties and work loads, clientele, and community settings vary widely. However, the number and variety of training plans developed, experiences documented, and manuals written during the 1960s and 1970s provide evidence about the kinds of training deemed helpful and important and related to effective job performance (U.S. Department of Labor, 1968; U.S. Department of Health, Education, and Welfare, 1974).

Training manuals and workbooks for new paraprofessionals have been developed regarding generic issues related to the world of work, individual and group behavior, community relationships, and worker development. Two kinds of paraprofessional service are usually proposed: assistance to people served by an agency and assistance to professionals in the field. Regardless of the diversity of worker's roles in terms of responsibility and job routines, the manuals focus on entry-level training and progressive on-the-job learning, continued in-service career development, and mobility.

Training developed within employing agencies is more comprehensive in some than in others. For example, fewer than one half of the New York school districts using paraprofessionals in 1969 provided a training program through their own resources or in concert with other institutions and organizations (New

York State Education Department, 1969, p. 1). And a two-county, two-college study in upstate New York (Wright, n.d.) indicates that most agencies involved gave minimal attention to the nature and amount of training needed by their parapro-fessionals. Training ranged from infrequent on-the-job counsel-ing and orientation sessions to orientation and ongoing in-service education. Some agencies provided released time to attend extramural courses; a few reimbursed tuition expenses or en-couraged further study by using course completion as a basis for some type of promotion.

Federal programs like Head Start, Community Action, and others initially developed a training component as part of their paraprofessional support. A major example is the expanded food and nutrition education program for limited resource fam-ilies sponsored, since 1968, through state Cooperative Exten-sion and supported by the U.S. Department of Agriculture. Fac-ulty in land-grant colleges, with responsibility for extension and continuing education, provide in-service education, teaching materials, and evaluative processes that enable professional staff at each of the program sites to recruit, select, and train parapro-fessionals residing in the community. Initial training focuses on the acquisition of subject matter, development of primary teach-ing and learning skills, and agency orientation. It is followed by group in-service training and individual counseling on the work of these new extension employees with the community's target population.

Colleges and universities have been especially involved in the education of professionals working with paraprofessionals; in designing programs for entry-level human service employ-ment, offering academic credit for lifelong learning, and devel-oping appropriate instructional programs for paraprofessionals (New Human Services Institute, 1975); and in researching vari-ous phases of programs employing paraprofessionals. A number of independent training institutes and institutes attached to aca-demic institutions, for example, the National Institute for New Careers, mobilized resources in the 1960s to supplement or carry out the limited personnel development services of employ-ing agencies. They proffered consultation, development of materials and procedures, technical advice and training teams, along with a multiplicity of methodology. The professions, too, became involved as legislation was enacted and funds made available. Guidelines and certification processes were developed along with training recommendations.

The training principle, which is supported by the National Institute for New Careers (U.S. Department of Labor, 1968), emphasizes learning linked to experience: immediate on-the-job training supplemented by remedial and course training related to the general issues of providing human services. Training under this principle includes preservice, on-the-job, and in-service training; opportunities for advancement; and career lattices that show how skills and knowledge can be applied in a variety of settings as economic conditions and job markets change.

Models for Training Plans

Most paraprofessional training plans are based on the characteristics of the trainees and the nature of the jobs they are to perform. Much of the literature calls for a clear specification of needs, training objectives, and job descriptions. In the early and basic planning of a paraprofessional training program decisions must be made about the skills, attitudes, and procedures that will comprise the training; methods and procedures to be used; amount of preservice training paraprofessionals will need before they can begin to offer program services; and type of in-service training they will receive.

Orientation training plans usually concentrate on developing a trainee's understanding of the work situation. Orientation serves several useful functions. It acquaints the trainee with the work situation, the goals and structure of the agency, the basic rules and policies, and the organization's expectations for employees. It also may identify trainees who have difficulty in adapting to the work situation, provide trainees with an opportunity to adjust to the idea of themselves as agency workers, and deal with logistical problems associated with work, like arranging for childcare and transportation (U.S. Department of Health, Education, and Welfare, 1974). In a sense, orientation is short-term training that enables program leaders to evaluate a trainee's skills, attitudes, and abilities to function effectively on a daily basis. Some work skills taught during orientation give entering workers a sense of adequacy.

Core training usually designates the development of basic functional skills needed to perform a job. Although core training is one of the most frequently used terms in the literature on paraprofessional training, there is still little agreement among authors and planners on its objectives, content, or methods. The focus in core training is often on the knowledge, skills, and attitudes considered necessary for all paraprofessionals and includes the following topics: policies, procedures, and organization of the agency; ethical issues such as confidentiality; community, cooperative, and organizational skills that enable one to use other paraprofessionals and groups as consultants and for support; and interpersonal skills.

In-service education, often called on-the-job training, at times is considered an extension of the core, but sometimes involves training in the specific content requirements of a job. These requirements include those most easily learned on the work site, such as agency procedures and position-specific skills. During in-service education that is intended as an extension of selected aspects of core training, the employee is no longer a trainee but a worker. Such training is usually conducted by agency supervisors or other staff, and the emphasis is on immediate job-related skills or problems. Although informal in-service methods may work satisfactorily, they should not be the only training procedures lest paraprofessionals find it difficult to recognize their complete roles in the larger setting and understand the organization and its management. In-service education coupled with regular supervision by and consultation with professional staff, however, will allow paraprofessionals to develop their skills and to understand their strengths and limitations.

Both core and position-specific training often rely on a basic model, especially in the teaching of selected skills: explanation of the skill, demonstration of the skill, practice of the skill with feedback in the training sessions until minimum competence is achieved, and practice of the skill with supervision in an actual work situation. The specificity of paraprofessional

training objectives varies greatly. Some program plans have generic guidelines that provide few specific objectives for program
operation, while others have fairly detailed operational objectives. Still others appear not to have stated any objectives. Goals
are most frequently stated in general terms that provide few suggestions for evaluation criteria. However, training programs proposed for those public agencies having adopted the concept of
paraprofessionalism as a career usually have specific operational
objectives for various segments of training (U.S. Department of
Health, Education, and Welfare, 1974).

Most designers of training programs feel that structured
classroom situations ought to be avoided, particularly with paraprofessionals from disadvantaged backgrounds. Participatory
and experiential learning is often recommended as well as early
fieldwork—learning by doing, role playing, and job simulation.
The length of training programs appears to depend on how
much paraprofessionals need to know before they can actually
begin work in an agency. Many programs tend to provide a
minimum amount of preservice training to involve paraprofessionals as quickly as possible in the agency's work. This goal
usually can be accomplished quite easily if the work required
permits paraprofessionals to perform initial tasks while learning
more complex or advanced skills for other portions of their
work.

Wright (n.d.) reports that organizations most likely to in-
vest in both preservice and planned continuing education are
those attempting to demonstrate the efficacy of developing previously disadvantaged persons, agencies such as Community
Action, Head Start, and Cooperative Extension. She also
notes that in organizations committed to developing disadvantaged trainees for career placement in human services, indicators
of job stability and career opportunity were positive. But in
some organizations not so committed, the employment of paraprofessionals seemed to be regarded as an interim measure to
slow down the escalation of service costs. Paraprofessionals ap-
peared concerned with receiving the kind of training that would
increase the life expectancy of their jobs and enhance their pos-
sibilities for promotion.

Morrill, Oetting, and Hurst (1974) propose an analysis of

current services that defines programs and services along three dimensions: the target of intervention, the purpose of the intervention, and the method of intervention. Such an analysis may assist agencies in deciding what their priorities of service are and areas in which paraprofessionals might most profitably be prepared and used (Delworth and Brown, 1977). The target dimension refers to interventions aimed at the individuals, their primary group, their associational groups, or the institutional or social groups that influence their behavior. The purpose dimension refers to the intent of the intervention: is it remedial, preventive, or developmental? The method, the third dimension, may be direct or indirect; that is, the paraprofessional may be directly involved in initiating and implementing the intervention, or indirectly involved through consultation and training of other paraprofessionals or through the use of media.

Recommendation for Extensive Training

To date there appear to be two selection processes, with meaningful differences, for entry into professional and many paraprofessional positions. Paraprofessional selection may emphasize the psychological make-up of candidates, while professional selection criteria are usually intellectual factors that may or may not correlate with effective interpersonal skills. Brown (1974) points out that paraprofessional training programs in counseling services tend to be homogeneous with a clear focus on competencies and attitudes necessary for the trainee's development. Professional preparation programs, in contrast, tend to be heterogeneous, involving science, art, research, and practice. Paraprofessional programs may emphasize communicative and facilitative skills in specific situations, while professional programs emphasize the trainee's development of discriminative skills. That the two types of programs reflect different training orientations can affect relationships in human service teams.

In systems that employ numerous paraprofessionals, difficulties related to the complex task of assessing the contributions of human service agencies often account for a scarcity of hard data. Few studies attempt to examine the relationships between characteristics of paraprofessionals and their clientele's success in reaching the program's objectives. Ostrander, Harding, and Cheney (1971) discovered, in a project in South Brooklyn sponsored by the Office of Economic Opportunity, that the fact that paraprofessionals were from the community did not guarantee that they would have the skills to establish rapport with community residents. They conclude that paraprofessionals need extensive training and close supportive supervision if their potential contributions are to be realized.

Feaster (1972) and Frye (1971) both demonstrate that the Cooperative Extension's expanded food and nutrition education program succeeded in reaching families with limited resources and in improving their food consumption practices. Yet Synectics Corporation (1971), on examining the program after a two-year initial effort, recommended that the role of the program's strongest asset—the paraprofessionals—be reexamined and attention paid to their training.

In an experimental study carried out in an inner-city community of New York, Yerka (1974) concludes that an assessment of training for paraprofessionals should be made at each program site because the competencies and judgment of individual professionals at each site may produce variations in training. In-service training should focus on the paraprofessionals' perceived needs for information and skills relevant to working with their clientele in addition to other job-related knowledge and skills. Finally, the study recommends that professionals and paraprofessionals need appropriate in-service training to supplement their skills in supervision and service, respectively. Paraprofessionals' knowledge of teaching and learning was found to be important to the success of their clients, and a standardized training approach to the acquisition of this knowledge was recommended. On-the-job performance ratings were most highly associated with criterion practice variables.

It is clear that the effective utilization of a paraprofessional staff calls for professional leadership. While relinquishing some traditional prerogatives, professionals retain primary responsibility for delivery of services. Professionals, administrators, and others must learn how to effectively utilize paraprofessionals' skills and develop their own management and supervisory skills. A major factor in the success of a professional-paraprofessional team is the former's skill in assigning and supervising the latter's activities.

Because most staff-level professionals have little or no training or experience in supervising auxiliary personnel, they need special preparation to help them understand the characteristics and culture of the paraprofessionals, the groups they represent, and their roles and functions; learn how to effectively utilize paraprofessionals' skills and knowledge; provide guidance and support as needed; and apply appropriate techniques of supervision, planning, and evaluation. In addition to the traditional role of being responsible for service to clients, professionals now often function as supervisors, trainers, and evaluators of other employees. Professionals may need guidance to develop the kind of professional-paraprofessional team relationship that will deliver optimum program services to clientele. Giving positive feedback or complimenting a paraprofessional is easily accomplished, but dealing with unsatisfactory performance requires facing a problem and dealing with it objectively, discussing problems openly, and suggesting ways for improvement. However, feedback on efforts and clear explanations of responsibilities may be much more important elements for paraprofessional than for professional job adjustment.

Professionals, trainers, and supervisors of paraprofessionals must identify paraprofessional job requirements and translate them into behavioral objectives, design training programs based on the activities required by the job, determine appropriate educational methods, select effective teaching materials and implement training programs, and evaluate the training programs. Very little of the present literature, however, examines the kind of preparation appropriate for those responsible for instructing paraprofessionals, other than an agreement that professionals should be prepared to work with paraprofessionals in personal and work relationships. Specific emphasis is usually placed on the orientation and perspective of entering paraprofessionals as well as their language and cognitive skills. Programs for professionals who implement paraprofessional training programs most often discuss paraprofessional characteristics and job tasks that take advantage of these, cultural styles, community relations, supervising techniques, coping with stress and anxieties, and criteria for judging competence and performance.

Workshops and conferences place the professional in the role of a trainer. Yet training is usually a shared learning process. While professionals share certified practice skills, paraprofessionals share their insights and skills gained through experience, on-the-job training, and knowledge of the clientele. Separate and joint sessions for paraprofessionals and professionals are necessary if staff members are to become integral members of human service teams. Separate sessions provide for specific needs of each group; joint sessions are essential to effective teamwork.

Assessment of Paraprofessionals' Effectiveness

Systematic attempts must be made to isolate some of the critical variables that account for successful utilization of paraprofessionals in community programs. One such study is a three-phase examination of the educational function of paraprofessionals in the Cooperative Extension nutrition program. In the first phase, Stuhlmiller (1973) developed, tested, and refined instruments to measure the progress of paraprofessionals toward three goals: knowledge and skill in working with families of limited resources, attitudes toward work, and job persistence. In the second phase, Engelbrecht (1972) examined the effect of the program on paraprofessionals and made recommendations for their recruitment and selection. In the third phase, Yerka (1974) explored the paraprofessionals' knowledge and understanding of the teaching-learning process, their attitudes toward assuming their role, and dimensions related to job persistence and performance in an inner-city community. The criteria against which achievement was measured were: success of families in reaching program objectives, level of desired practices attained, program information recalled, and recognition of assistance received by program clientele. This study provides evidence that it is possible to select, train, and place in the community paraprofessionals whose backgrounds are not too different from those of their clients. Paraprofessionals, who benefit from training and supervision, are able to establish relationships with clients who are generally considered difficult to reach and to work effectively with them.

More studies need to be conducted in which program goals, rather than process, are measured. Paraprofessionals' effectiveness in terms of contributing to their clients' success should be a focus of future research.

Implications for the Future

If human service agencies continue to support the use of professional-paraprofessional teams or partnerships, the agencies need to consider four sets of questions. First, what is the need for a paraprofessional program and what does the agency hope to accomplish by employing paraprofessionals? What functions will they perform? Are agency administrators, as well as educators, sufficiently specific about competence and the requirements of jobs in their agencies in order to develop realistic placements of workers?

Second, what support does the program have? Are paraprofessional functions seen as compatible with the agency's goals, philosophy, and structure? Are prospective paraprofessionals, potential consumers, agency professionals, administrators, and related groups interested? Third, what resources can the agency commit to the program? What investment does the agency envision making? How will paraprofessionals be recruited, trained, and supervised? What place will they occupy in the agency's personnel hierarchy? Fourth, what benefits accrue to the agency and paraprofessionals as a result of the latter's work? What criteria will be used to evaluate the effects of the paraprofessionals on the agency and the community? How will these decisions be made, and who will participate in making them? Will benefits be offset by resources needed to obtain, train, and supervise the new staff? When will benefits be observable?

Agencies must be committed to training professionals, paraprofessionals, and clients or consumers to understand the roles and functions of the agencies' paraprofessionals. Such planning requires analysis, time, and effort. Agencies that engage in careful and thoughtful planning are likely to conclude that paraprofessionals are not a panacea. On the contrary, paraprofessionals may bring an agency face-to-face with many of the deepest problems of our society, and confronting these problems may well be difficult (D'Onofrio, 1970). Plans for implementing a program's selection criteria, training design, and supervision procedures, as well as plans for evaluating paraprofessionals and implementing the programs and services in which they will be involved, have to be given high priority to assure efficient, realistic, and coordinated program operation.

An urgent question is the amount and type of training and supervision that produce maximal effectiveness; these specifications will determine how widely paraprofessionals should be trained and utilized. Agencies and researchers must undertake systematic, ongoing evaluations of training and supervision that serve to provide feedback to both paraprofessionals and professionals, determine whether specific training or service goals are being met, help agencies decide which paraprofessional services merit continued support and training, and increase training programs' credibility within the community and among top administrators (Delworth and Brown, 1977, p. 153). Thus a single program's effectiveness could be evaluated by the following criteria: job standards and observed trainee performance; program effect on clientele; supervisor's perception of the program's effects on trainees; trainees' perceptions of personal benefits from the program; job persistence, measured by absenteeism, tardiness, and turnover. Most activities required by these approaches can be performed by the trainer or supervisor.

Although the uninitiated may believe that paraprofessionals make a professional's job easier, that is not necessarily true. By assuming certain duties, paraprofessionals release professionals to initiate activities at a higher and broader level. As a result, the development of a professional-paraprofessional team can provide a more productive environment for learning, teaching, and service.

Chapter Five

Training
Volunteers

Stephen H. Confer

Trainers attempt to balance the needs, goals, and values of the sponsoring organizations with the needs, goals, and values of the trainers. Success in training, in its most realistic sense, is a measure of the ability of a trainer to effectively balance these items.

Today some 37 million persons are involved in some form of volunteer work. A survey indicated that 220,000 Retired Senior Volunteer Program members volunteered over 40,353,000 hours in community services during 1977 ("Over 40 Million Hours . . . ," 1978). Community, church, health, and labor organizations must all attract, train, utilize, and retain volunteers. The changing role of women in our society has affected volunteer organizations in that more women are entering full-time paid positions. Volunteer groups, such as health and community organizations, that were once dependent on nonemployed housewives as the source of their volunteers have seen that pool of able and eager workers dwindle and have had to develop new sources. However, organizations whose volunteer activities are associated with employment, such as unions, have seen an increasing number of women among their volunteers.

The result of this shift is that volunteers in any organization are bound to be increasingly diverse in their background. Laws prohibiting discrimination in employment on the basis of age and the declining numbers of young people will have additional effects on the diversity of the background of volunteers. So, too, are volunteer organizations changing. Federal, state, and local governments now assume responsibility for providing many of the services volunteers in health, welfare, and other independent organizations once provided. Additionally, government interest and activity have changed the relationship between the worker (whether blue-collar, professional, management, or clerical) and the employer, and thus, the nature of worker, professional, and management volunteer organizations.

There are three distinct categories of volunteer organizations. The first is that group of organizations generally not associated with the pursuit of economic goals or the world of work, such as churches, which have a membership from which they draw volunteers. The second category includes organizations such as the United Way which do not have individual memberships but operate through and within the business and industrial community and are generally dependent upon that community for volunteers. The third category comprises professional organizations and labor unions that have an economic or labor orientation and draw upon their membership for volunteers. In this chapter, we discuss the training of volunteers for all three types of volunteer organizations. Some specific points are more relevant to one category than to the others and these will be noted. Generally, training as applied to volunteer organizations is discussed relative to its success in balancing participant and organization needs, goals, and values in this environment of change.

Overview of Training Methods

It seems obvious that needs assessment should precede the development of a training program. In practice, however, most training organizations use needs assessment data that are subjective rather than objective, political rather than apolitical, and private rather than public. Often times, trainers in volunteer organizations are unable to collect original data on training needs and participant characteristics. Trainers of volunteers often find they must make intuitive assumptions about the participants in their programs and develop training based on second-hand information (nearly always an administrative directive to develop a specific program) and their own experience.

Although training based on administrative directives, personal experience, and assumptions is often acceptable to participants and administrators, this approach to the identification of human resources problems is not satisfactory to many trainers. To satisfy participants and administrators, trainers often find that they are expected to be entertainers. If they are particularly skillful entertainers, they may provide entertainment but little content, happiness but little intended behavior change, and their trainees may become committed to the trainer but not to the organization.

The trainer who must operate in such an environment will probably find it more rewarding to maintain the environment than to undertake its dismantling. However, when change is desired, trainers often find it useful to work with advisory or planning committees whose members include those agency personnel who have to live with the results of the training effort: trainers, supervisors of volunteers, and others with similar direct contact. Certainly, the establishment of a committee does not assure that human resources problems will be examined rationally. Such assurance can best be obtained if the professional trainer first teaches committee members about problem-solving processes. The trainer can present evaluative data regarding needs assessment and previous training programs, pointing out the gaps in those data and encouraging the committee to ask questions about training needs and participant characteristics.

Volunteer organizations use several other techniques—not unique to volunteer organizations—to assess training needs, for example, preconference questionnaires and participant expectation exercises. Preconference questionnaires are mailed to prospective participants before the training program begins; they must be mailed early enough to allow for response time and to be useful in planning the training program. The questionnaire may ask participants to list the skills they feel should be included in the training, and to indicate the importance of these skills by rank ordering the list. Such questionnaires are most valuable for participants who have some experience in the particular area of volunteer work in which they are to be trained, as their experience provides a basis for informed answers.

Participant expectation exercises can be conducted at the first training session. Such exercises can inform the trainer about which subject areas the participants anticipate learning, and the exercises may allay anxiety among participants concerning the particular areas that will indeed be covered. The process is simple enough, involving only a brief request by the trainer that all participants arrive at the first training session with expectations as to what is going to take place and what the atmosphere will be. At the first session, the trainer asks the participants to name those expectations they have and lists them on newsprint. Once the list is completed, the trainer can go over each item and identify when during the training the item will be discussed, add items of particularly strong interest that were not originally included in the training plan, and arrange individual opportunities to cover items not in the plan that concern only a few participants. This expectation list should be referred to throughout the training to assure everyone that the program is responding to the participants' stated needs. At the end of the program, reference to the list will assure that each item was covered by the trainer.

Volunteer organizations, like other organizations, have tried a full range of training techniques. Programmed instruction, lectures, demonstrations, role playing, group discussions, and other techniques all have their supporters among the trainers of volunteers. There is, however, some consistency among volunteer trainers concerning the techniques that work best for them. Among the techniques they find most effective are group discussion, simulation, demonstration, and small-group or large-group work. Among the techniques they find least effective are lengthy lectures and presentations that do not actively involve the trainees.

It is appropriate here to discuss one element that is more important in the training of volunteers than in the training of other kinds of participants. This element is the ceremonial effect, which refers to those parts of the training that do not aim to develop volunteers' skills but rather to encourage their identification with the volunteer organization. Fraternal organizations have always recognized the need for ceremony. Many volunteer organizations make efforts in this area but often without sufficient recognition of the objective of those efforts. The distribution of certificates at graduation luncheons is a ceremonial activity in training, as is the wearing of lapel pins and other insignia and recognition patches.

The trainer of volunteers should carefully plan ceremonial activities related to training and evaluate their effectiveness. Ceremonial activities should be as carefully planned as all other parts of a training program for volunteers. The trainer should carefully think through the program's objectives and devise ceremonial activities throughout the program, not merely at its conclusion. Ceremony increases volunteers' identification with the organization and provides opportunities for the volunteers to become personally familiar with the organization's structure, operation, and personalities.

Probably the most important consideration is that ceremonial activities should be of a form that encourages volunteers to identify the organization as a source of good feelings or positive reinforcement. Volunteers' achievements and group identification should be reinforced by the leadership and the staff of the organization. Reinforcement increases the probability that the reinforced behavior will occur again and most likely with increasing frequency. By reinforcing volunteers' achievements, the organization enhances the good feelings volunteers normally have about their accomplishments. By reinforcing group identi-

n tends to measure how participants feel about the program
her than how much they learn. For example, trainers of vol-
teers often seek to measure the success of their programs by
king the trainees whether they found the program enjoyable
d asking them how the training could have been improved.
e net effect of this approach to evaluation is that the trainer
tains a fairly good picture of how the participants feel about
training but little or no information on how the training in-
ences the behavior of the participants or the effectiveness of
organization.

There are three other approaches to evaluating training
ograms. First, cognitive approaches measure the changes in
skills and knowledge of the participants that occur as a re-
t of training. Pretests and posttests—or before and after mea-
es of skills and knowledge—are the usual means for determin-
cognitive changes. The trainer should be aware that volunteers
y associate tests with unpleasant experiences such as failure
being identified as less able or competent than others. Volun-
rs may cease participating if the volunteer organization be-
mes a source of such unpleasant experiences. As there are too
v active volunteers at present, no trainer of volunteers should
pose unpleasant mechanisms such as tests. However, pre- and
stmeasures can be used as long as the trainer selects measures
t do not create the unpleasantness most adults associate with
ts. For example, tests that are submitted anonymously may
used. Immediate feedback of the results can be effective in
owing participants that the cognitive measures are valuable
ols for improving their training. Pre- and posttests should be
corporated into the program as a part of the actual learning
perience. While the use of anonymous tests affects the data
cording in any evaluation, this apparent disadvantage must be
ighed against the feelings of the volunteers about tests.

A second approach to evaluating the effectiveness of a
ining program involves observations of the behavior of the
rticipants after the training sessions. The trainer can observe
the volunteers are applying the skills presented in the training
they work for the organization. However, whether or not the
sired behaviors are in evidence, the trainer should be cautious

fication, the organization encourages volunteers to return to
that group to receive further reinforcement as well as satisfaction from group activities. The process of binding volunteers
to an organization is at least as important as the skill and knowledge components of volunteer training. Effective binding will
minimize turnover among volunteers.

Volunteers' Sociocentricity

From conducting a small number of interviews with trainers, I find that training methods that use participatory activities
are deemed most effective by them. This finding suggests that
volunteers seem to learn best from group-oriented activities
that provide some opportunity for social interaction. If this
conclusion is correct, it in turn suggests two hypotheses: (1)
Volunteers tend to be more sociocentric than egocentric; and
(2) Volunteers tend to prefer training programs that emphasize
group activity. Let us examine each of these hypotheses.

Volunteers evidence behavior that is less concerned with
the individual self than with a group or the larger society. Interviews with trainers of volunteers support this view. Volunteers
are consistently described as "being concerned with belonging,
with being accepted," and as disinclined to "disregard the feelings of others and look out for themselves" (Confer, 1980).

In studying workers' motivation to work, Hertzberg
(1966) distinguishes two sets of factors. Hygiene factors are extrinsic to the work itself and include salary, interpersonal relationships, status, technical supervision, organization policy,
physical working conditions, the effect of the job on personal
life, and job security. Hertzberg hypothesizes that such hygiene
factors do not serve to motivate by their presence, but rather
they function as dissatisfiers if they are not present or not present in sufficient quantity. In contrast, Hertzberg considers intrinsic factors such as achievement, recognition, and possible
growth as motivating factors.

A study (Confer, 1971) of eighty-two full-time union
staff members appointed from among the volunteer leadership
to work with volunteers, however, shows that Hertzberg's analy-

Stephen H. Confer

sis of workers cannot be directly applied to volunteers. Because the staff members were volunteers once, their responses should not differ significantly from current volunteers. When asked to identify the times they felt very good about their job and to indicate the factors present at those times, the respondents identified achievement (present in 97 percent of the situations in which they felt best), recognition (71 percent), work itself (91 percent), and responsibility (95 percent). Normally considered as motivators, advancement and possible growth were only mentioned for 33 percent and 32 percent, respectively, of the best situations (Confer, 1980).

Of greater interest to the trainer of volunteers, however, is the fact that three items normally considered only as hygiene factors were major motivators for this group—relationships with subordinates (92 percent), relationship with superiors (89 percent), and relationships with peers (97 percent). Additionally, when these factors were present in a situation in which respondents felt good about their jobs, the respondents indicated that the presence of these factors was very important to them (Confer, 1980).

Such data support our hypothesis that volunteers tend to be sociocentric. We may now consider data that support our second hypothesis, that volunteers tend to prefer training programs that emphasize group activities. Evaluation data were collected by a labor union on two training programs attended during 1974 by 446 volunteers (Confer, 1975). These programs were conducted at various universities and consisted of courses devoted largely to group-oriented activities and courses that emphasized lectures or other instructor-dominated activities.

The first training program was attended by 304 volunteers and consisted of three group-oriented courses (concepts of leadership, communications skills, and human relations) and six instructor-dominated courses (building an effective local, doing legislative work, doing political work, labor economics, labor law, and organizing). When the participants were asked which course they found most useful, 62.5 percent named one of the group-oriented subjects.

The second training program was attended by 142 volunteers and consisted of three group-oriented courses (commit-

ment with action, communications dynamics, tions) and two instructor-dominated courses (work and doing political work). Again the p asked which course was the most useful, a named one of the group-oriented courses. This gests that training techniques that involve volu or relate to groups are preferred by volunteers niques that are more individual in nature or do social interaction.

There are two precautions, however, in any training technique to volunteer training. need to see the immediate application of the not inclined to attend training or to participa which they see no use. Second, just as no two training session with the same value system o two training groups or volunteer organizatio value system or set of needs. For example, oped programmed instruction material to be u teers to quickly attain a minimum level of co 1975). In each case, the material was well de laid out, and based on problems and processes ered to be important. Both sets were clearly small steps and immediate feedback. One uni mediate success with the program, while the number of complaints, and few of its volu program. That union redesigned the mate steps, added audio material and graphics, a out and design. Although the first union c cessful with its material, the second union material to be still unsuccessful. Evaluative union's training advisory committee finally the new volunteers nor the administrators the aspect of studying alone. The program dropped by that union but continues succ

Evaluating Training Progr

For the most part, the evaluation programs is affective rather than cognitive

in attributing any change or the lack of it to the training program. It is possible that competing behaviors are reinforced on
the job and the behaviors learned during training are not.

A third approach to evaluation is the use of organizational measures such as the number of clients serviced, grievances
won, and other such data normally collected by organizations.
Such measures may be used to compare the performance of
those individuals or groups who have had training and those
who have not. Any comparison of this sort must take into consideration other, extraneous variables that may increase or reduce any differences between the two groups. Extraneous variables cannot be controlled for, and their identification may
prove quite difficult. However, the use of organizational measures is helpful in determining whether training has, in fact, enabled volunteers to demonstrate the competencies the training
was designed to help them achieve.

The professional trainer of volunteers needs some measure of the effectiveness of training and should select the technique or combination of techniques that is most effective in
evaluating the particular training and is consistent with various
constraints. Too, it is possible that affective measures provide
more information than they are normally given credit for. Often
an affective measure is the only one available to the trainer,
given organizational and political constraints. Therefore, affective measures should be carefully studied to determine their
value relative to cognitive, organizational, and behavioral measures. One comparative study collected affective and cognitive
data on 749 participants in a union training program (Confer,
1973). Due to the organizational constraint of privacy, it was
not possible to keep the data in such a form that individual cognitive and affective data could be matched. However, the average cognitive and affective scores for each of the ten training
sites were calculated; the difference between the mean pre- and
posttest scores positively correlated with the mean affective
scores ($r = .69$, significant at .05 level; Confer, 1980).

These results suggest the need for further research on the
interpretation and use of affective measures in the evaluation of
training. If it is found that achievement consistently covaries

with feelings toward the training and that variance in achievement can be predicted from affective measures, then the use of
affective measures would take on much greater significance in
the evaluation of training. Affective measures are also important
in that they may reveal factors responsible for turnover among
volunteers.

As mentioned earlier, evaluation can also be used as part
of the training itself by using a pretest to make participants
aware of the organization's or trainer's expectations and a diagnostic posttest to assist trainers and participants in assessing individuals' training needs. Evaluation can also be used to reinforce the training and new behaviors back on the job. This purpose can be accomplished through a series of follow-up questionnaires. The first follow-up asks if the participants use the skills
they learned; the second asks them to describe instances in
which they use the skills; and the third asks for the results or evaluation of the efforts undertaken using the particular skills.

Individualizing Training

An ideal training program for volunteers contains components that provide for the fullest possible meshing of individual
volunteer's needs with the needs of the volunteer organization.
Participants learn best in an environment in which they feel free
to learn those things that they believe will benefit themselves
and their organization. Thus the trainer must be able to adjust
a general training method to the specific needs of the participants and the organization. Interviews and surveys are the most
effective devices for individualizing a program for a specific audience. Interview and survey data enable the trainer to select
the techniques best suited to the volunteers, the organization,
and the skills to be learned. The higher the level of complexity
of the skills, the greater the utility of counseling and interviewing in contrast to surveying. Conversely, trainers whose programs involve highly structured and straightforward skills will
find surveys and pretests to be most useful in the determination
of training techniques.

Similarly, the selection of appropriate training techniques

depends on the nature of the training, the size and diversity of the group to be trained, the felt needs of the volunteers, and the needs identified by the organization. Considerations such as money and politics also affect the selection of training techniques. As noted earlier, the same basic technique (in that case, programmed instruction) can have highly divergent results even though used in organizations that appear similar. Let us review one piece of research that can assist trainers in selecting the appropriate training technique for a particular group of volunteers.

Graves (1966) identifies a series of value systems that operate in our society. Each set of values represents a "level of existence," and each level "is a state of equilibrium through which people pass on the way to other states of equilibrium"; at "a particular level of existence, a person has a psychology which is particular and peculiar to that level" (p. 121). A person's acts, feelings, motivations, ethics, values, and thoughts result in behaviors intended to solve the problems and conflicts associated with a given level. For our purposes, it is most important to note that persons at a particular level tend to prefer particular styles of leadership and training techniques.

Graves identifies seven levels, six of which are relevant to noninstitutionalized adults in contemporary western society:

1. Tribalistic: Persons at this level prefer to stay with their own kind of people, and work for a fair and friendly boss; they follow long-established and traditional ways of doing things.
2. Egocentric: Persons at this level tend to look out for themselves first; they value power and the active exercise of it.
3. Conformist: Persons at this level are bureaucratic; rules, regulations, standards, and instructions guide their behavior.
4. Manipulative: Persons at this level value game playing; prestige, respect, and physical trappings are important to them.
5. Sociocentric: Persons at this level value group activity and belonging.
6. Existential: Persons at this level are spontaneous and free from the constraints that inhibit most others; the challenge of tough goals and the freedom to pursue them are strong motivators.

For each level, we can suggest a training style or set of techniques that is most compatible: (1) tribalistic—sermonizing; (2) egocentric—direct orders and specific instruction; (3) conformist—programming including all details; (4) manipulative—lecture and discussion; (5) sociocentric—group activities; and (6) existential—individualized activities directed toward agreed objectives.

As noted earlier, volunteers are likely to be sociocentric; it appears that a sociocentric value system is more in keeping with the nature of volunteer work. However, the trainer of volunteers should not take the sociocentric nature of volunteers as a given but rather should separately assess each individual and group. Thus, the trainer can adopt techniques most compatible with the value system of the volunteers.

Training should also be adapted to the organization in which the volunteers are to work. Many leaders of volunteer organizations are inclined to assume that their volunteers are fully aware of the organization's goals and needs, that such awareness prompted them to volunteer. Leaders of volunteer organizations, however, tend to shape those organizations to meet their own needs and express their own value systems. As a result, misunderstandings may arise among leaders and groups of volunteers new to the organization.

Organizational goals and needs can be stated in orientation sessions to provide an initial opportunity for new volunteers and established leaders to explore them together. However, orientation sessions are often insufficient to fully integrate new volunteers. Volunteers need more individualized goal identification sessions that provide opportunities for each volunteer to identify congruencies between personal goals and organizational goals. The trainer must establish the environment and processes wherein volunteers in training programs can compare and match their needs, goals, and values to those of the organization.

Individualized training is needed to supplement a group training program because the wide variety of needs and values among volunteers assures that classroom training alone cannot meet all volunteers' needs. Thus the fullest possible use of individualization is almost a necessity. Further, when appropriate, a broad range of community resources can be used to advantage. Local meetings, conventions, and other opportunities seemingly unrelated to training activities can be incorporated into the training program. The opportunity for the volunteer to learn and to grow through volunteer activity can be facilitated through individualization and the identification and legitimization of activities usually unassociated with training. The legitimization of skills and knowledge learned outside the traditional system is sure to benefit the volunteer, the trainer, and the volunteer organization.

In sum, the trainer of volunteers should be concerned with how the participants can best learn as well as what the participants actually learn. Volunteers will learn the skills and knowledge that they perceive as serving their needs, goals, and values. They cannot be forced to learn what they do not want to learn nor what they do not perceive as having relevance to their volunteer activities. It is incumbent upon the trainer of volunteers, therefore, to assist in the thorough exploration of the needs, goals, and values shared by the organization and individual volunteers. The larger that common area, the greater the potential for volunteers' growth through volunteer activity, the more readily volunteers will participate, and the more thorough the integration of volunteers into the volunteer organization.

Ideal Training Program

To demonstrate the elements of an ideal training program for volunteers, it is useful to present an example that is, in small part, hypothetical. But let us first make a basic assumption about the volunteer organization and the volunteers. For situations to which some aspect of this assumption does not apply, the example must be adjusted appropriately. Our assumption is: The volunteers are able to attend an intensive full-time program either because they are not otherwise employed, their employer allows for this time off the job, or the volunteer organization subsidizes participation.

The general objectives of our model training program are

(1) to provide the greatest possible opportunity for participants to identify and learn those skills and knowledge that will be most useful to them as volunteers; (2) to establish an environment wherein participants will be able to test perceived constraints on their ability to perform and to learn; and (3) to reinforce participants' behavioral change from teacher-dependent learners to independent learners.

The first portion of the program is an orientation to the program and establishes the rules and guidelines. More important, some time is spent identifying and examining all individual learning styles and legitimizing individual preferences. Resources available to participants are examined and discussed, including, as appropriate, classroom time, audiotapes and videotapes, books and articles, and community facilities. The trainer explains and demonstrates that all participants are expected to develop performance objectives for their volunteer work and, from those, or from a list of options, to identify instructional objectives. For each appropriate training period, the participants are expected to submit learning contracts specifying the instructional objectives they intend to use (such as formal classroom, written, video, audio, or tutorial) and how they plan to evaluate their accomplishment.

At the end of the orientation, the participants will have analyzed their performance objectives, identified a manageable number of instructional objectives, and submitted their first learning contract to the trainer. A learning contract is simply an agreement between the trainers and an individual participant consisting of five items: (1) the learning objectives to be attained; (2) the activities the participant plans to use to attain each objective; (3) the method for evaluating the attainment of each objective; (4) the assistance, if any, needed from the trainer or the organization to attain each objective; and (5) the length of time for the completion of the contract. In addition, small common-interest support groups will have been formed that will later submit a group project (such as a training program, slide show, or paper) that offers material which the volunteers can directly apply to their volunteer activities.

Following the period of orientation, the trainer should

suggest a selection of short but timely training activities congruent with the individual learning contracts and organizational needs. The selection of topic areas for these sessions should be derived from an examination of the volunteers' performance objectives and learning contracts as well as the organization's objectives. The trainer can be assured that the selected topic areas do indeed fit organizational needs if the correspondences between organizational and individual needs are thoroughly clarified. With appropriate negotiation and counseling, the volunteers' learning contracts will reflect those correspondences. Of course, certain instructional objectives in specific topic areas may be mandatory, independent of the learning contracts. However, the trainer should make explicit the rationale for any mandatory objectives or topics. The trainer should also remind volunteers that it is the attainment of the instructional objectives that is important—not necessarily how they are attained. Tutorials, on-the-job training, attendance at meetings or conventions, and the completion of special projects are all legitimate means for volunteers to attain their learning objectives.

The trainer may wish to explore the possibility of awarding continuing education units for successful completion of instructional objectives. The trainer may be able to develop a relationship with a local university or community college that will result in the awarding of credits for the volunteers' efforts. Too, the American Council on Education has sponsored a project to examine the internal training programs of various organizations and to recommend the awarding of credits should those who complete these programs wish to make such application to a university or a community college in the future. Recognition of this type is important to volunteers as it legitimizes volunteer experience for future job-related efforts. This legitimization of volunteer work is a major concern of the largest group of volunteers, women, as many of them find it necessary to enter the paid labor force.

It is apparent that the role of the trainer in a program such as that just described is critical. In more traditional programs, the bulk of the trainer's effort and time is spent in actual instruction before a group. In the design just described, the trainer spends considerably more time as a consultant or counselor to the participants. The development of realistic performance objectives, the identification and writing of instructional objectives, and the preparation of learning contracts are only part of the additional effort required. The participants also need some guidance in identifying resources and in overcoming and discovering barriers to their learning. Some participants may initially resent the trainer's untraditional role. Most traditional educational experiences are teacher-oriented rather than learner-oriented, and learners may initially be frustrated or confused by being held responsible for their learning. That frustration can be turned to enthusiasm through skilled counseling.

The trainer who attempts to implement an ideal program will find that the majority of his or her time will be spent in problem-solving or counseling activities. The focus of these activities should be to assist the organization's leaders and staff in identifying and solving human resources problems. Under no circumstances should the trainer identify the program and then attempt to identify the problems to which it can be applied. Rather, the trainer best serves the organization by asking questions before implementing programs requested by leaders. Each training program should be designed to solve a specific problem that is, by its nature, solvable by training.

Training advisory committees can help a trainer implement a problem-solving approach. It is standard practice, however, to have a trainer submit schedules of training programs and outlines of proposed programs to the committee. This procedure should be avoided. The committee should rather examine organizational studies and diagnoses and indexes of human resources problems. The evaluation data from earlier training programs should also be available to members of training advisory committees.

Those who serve on training advisory committees may have training responsibilities in other organizations in which they are volunteers. Thus, these members' experiences, skills, and training may well be useful in implementing a problem-solving approach to training. Advisory committee members' needs, as volunteers, should not be overlooked. Their service on the committee should provide them with an opportunity to improve their own skills. If committee meetings provide learning opportunities for committee members, such meetings will improve the members' skills, bind the members closer to the organization, and assure that the members consider the necessary data for problem solving in the volunteer organization.

Trainers in volunteer organizations have the opportunity to become recognized as professionals. Their development, the attainment of a full range of skills for human resources development, is critical to this process. Greater opportunities for creative application of these skills are available in volunteer organizations than in any other setting. Trainers in volunteer organizations soon find that the effective development of human resources is not a function of the dollars spent on a development program but rather of the trainer's creativity, intelligence, and abilities.

Summary

Information regarding the human resources of a volunteer organization is the most powerful tool in a trainer's tool kit. Data regarding these resources may be collected during formal and informal discussions with the organization's leaders, staff, and volunteers. Surveys are another source of such information and should be used when appropriate. The examination of organizational performance data often provides clues to human resources problems. Once the data are collected, the trainer should be able to analyze that data and derive hypotheses about the organization's human resources needs. These analyses should be distributed and be used as the basis for further discussion. Evaluation data should also be distributed and shared.

The trainer in a volunteer organization who pursues the recommendations made in this chapter will first concentrate on organizational problems and the needs, goals, and values of the volunteers; then develop training activities that will serve the organization and the volunteers' shared needs; and, finally, use methods of evaluation appropriate to the situation.

Chapter Six

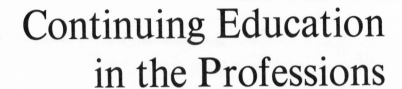

Continuing Education in the Professions

Stanley M. Grabowski

Continuing education in the professions is distinct from preservice preparation for a profession, although there is a connection between them. Among researchers, however, there is no agreement on what constitutes a profession, despite numerous attempts at definition (Flexner, 1915; DeLancy, 1938; Hughes, 1962; Wilensky, 1964; Vollmer and Mills, 1966; Boyette, Blount, and Petaway, 1971; Schein and Kommers, 1972; Anderson, 1974; Mayhew and Ford, 1974; Rose, 1974; Nyre and Reilly, 1979). In this chapter, *profession* is used in the broadest possible sense to include any occupation designated as a profession by any authoritative source such as investigative researchers, the Bureau of Labor Statistics, and the National Center for Education Statistics. *Continuing education* refers to any and all fication, the organization encourages volunteers to return to that group to receive further reinforcement as well as satisfaction from group activities. The process of binding volunteers to an organization is at least as important as the skill and knowledge components of volunteer training. Effective binding will minimize turnover among volunteers.

Volunteers' Sociocentricity

From conducting a small number of interviews with trainers, I find that training methods that use participatory activities are deemed most effective by them. This finding suggests that volunteers seem to learn best from group-oriented activities that provide some opportunity for social interaction. If this conclusion is correct, it in turn suggests two hypotheses: (1) Volunteers tend to be more sociocentric than egocentric; and (2) Volunteers tend to prefer training programs that emphasize group activity. Let us examine each of these hypotheses.

Volunteers evidence behavior that is less concerned with the individual self than with a group or the larger society. Interviews with trainers of volunteers support this view. Volunteers are consistently described as "being concerned with belonging, with being accepted," and as disinclined to "disregard the feelings of others and look out for themselves" (Confer, 1980).

In studying workers' motivation to work, Hertzberg (1966) distinguishes two sets of factors. Hygiene factors are extrinsic to the work itself and include salary, interpersonal relationships, status, technical supervision, organization policy, physical working conditions, the effect of the job on personal life, and job security. Hertzberg hypothesizes that such hygiene factors do not serve to motivate by their presence, but rather they function as dissatisfiers if they are not present or not present in sufficient quantity. In contrast, Hertzberg considers intrinsic factors such as achievement, recognition, and possible growth as motivating factors.

A study (Confer, 1971) of eighty-two full-time union staff members appointed from among the volunteer leadership to work with volunteers, however, shows that Hertzberg's analysis of workers cannot be directly applied to volunteers. Because the staff members were volunteers once, their responses should not differ significantly from current volunteers. When asked to identify the times they felt very good about their job and to indicate the factors present at those times, the respondents identified achievement (present in 97 percent of the situations in which they felt best), recognition (71 percent), work itself (91 percent), and responsibility (95 percent). Normally considered as motivators, advancement and possible growth were only mentioned for 33 percent and 32 percent, respectively, of the best situations (Confer, 1980).

Of greater interest to the trainer of volunteers, however, is the fact that three items normally considered only as hygiene factors were major motivators for this group—relationships with subordinates (92 percent), relationship with superiors (89 percent), and relationships with peers (97 percent). Additionally, when these factors were present in a situation in which respondents felt good about their jobs, the respondents indicated that the presence of these factors was very important to them (Confer, 1980).

Such data support our hypothesis that volunteers tend to be sociocentric. We may now consider data that support our second hypothesis, that volunteers tend to prefer training programs that emphasize group activities. Evaluation data were collected by a labor union on two training programs attended during 1974 by 446 volunteers (Confer, 1975). These programs were conducted at various universities and consisted of courses devoted largely to group-oriented activities and courses that emphasized lectures or other instructor-dominated activities.

The first training program was attended by 304 volunteers and consisted of three group-oriented courses (concepts of leadership, communications skills, and human relations) and six instructor-dominated courses (building an effective local, doing legislative work, doing political work, labor economics, labor law, and organizing). When the participants were asked which course they found most useful, 62.5 percent named one of the group-oriented subjects.

The second training program was attended by 142 volunteers and consisted of three group-oriented courses (commitment with action, communications dynamics, and human relations) and two instructor-dominated courses (doing legislative work and doing political work). Again the participants were asked which course was the most useful, and 69.6 percent named one of the group-oriented courses. This information suggests that training techniques that involve volunteers as a group or relate to groups are preferred by volunteers to training techniques that are more individual in nature or do not permit some social interaction.

There are two precautions, however, in the application of any training technique to volunteer training. First, volunteers need to see the immediate application of the training; they are not inclined to attend training or to participate in exercises for which they see no use. Second, just as no two people arrive at a training session with the same value system or set of needs, no two training groups or volunteer organizations have the same value system or set of needs. For example, two unions developed programmed instruction material to be used by new volunteers to quickly attain a minimum level of competency (Confer, 1975). In each case, the material was well designed, attractively laid out, and based on problems and processes volunteers considered to be important. Both sets were clearly programmed with small steps and immediate feedback. One union experienced immediate success with the program, while the second received a number of complaints, and few of its volunteers finished the program. That union redesigned the material, created larger steps, added audio material and graphics, and modified the layout and design. Although the first union continued to be successful with its material, the second union found its modified material to be still unsuccessful. Evaluative responses from the union's training advisory committee finally revealed that neither the new volunteers nor the administrators of the program liked the aspect of studying alone. The programmed instruction was dropped by that union but continues successfully in the other.

Evaluating Training Programs

For the most part, the evaluation of volunteer training programs is affective rather than cognitive; that is, such evaluation tends to measure how participants feel about the program rather than how much they learn. For example, trainers of volunteers often seek to measure the success of their programs by asking the trainees whether they found the program enjoyable and asking them how the training could have been improved. The net effect of this approach to evaluation is that the trainer obtains a fairly good picture of how the participants feel about the training but little or no information on how the training influences the behavior of the participants or the effectiveness of the organization.

There are three other approaches to evaluating training programs. First, cognitive approaches measure the changes in the skills and knowledge of the participants that occur as a result of training. Pretests and posttests—or before and after measures of skills and knowledge—are the usual means for determining cognitive changes. The trainer should be aware that volunteers may associate tests with unpleasant experiences such as failure or being identified as less able or competent than others. Volunteers may cease participating if the volunteer organization becomes a source of such unpleasant experiences. As there are too few·active volunteers at present, no trainer of volunteers should impose unpleasant mechanisms such as tests. However, pre- and postmeasures can be used as long as the trainer selects measures that do not create the unpleasantness most adults associate with tests. For example, tests that are submitted anonymously may be used. Immediate feedback of the results can be effective in showing participants that the cognitive measures are valuable tools for improving their training. Pre- and posttests should be incorporated into the program as a part of the actual learning experience. While the use of anonymous tests affects the data recording in any evaluation, this apparent disadvantage must be weighed against the feelings of the volunteers about tests.

A second approach to evaluating the effectiveness of a training program involves observations of the behavior of the participants after the training sessions. The trainer can observe if the volunteers are applying the skills presented in the training as they work for the organization. However, whether or not the desired behaviors are in evidence, the trainer should be cautious

in attributing any change or the lack of it to the training program. It is possible that competing behaviors are reinforced on the job and the behaviors learned during training are not.

A third approach to evaluation is the use of organizational measures such as the number of clients serviced, grievances won, and other such data normally collected by organizations. Such measures may be used to compare the performance of those individuals or groups who have had training and those who have not. Any comparison of this sort must take into consideration other, extraneous variables that may increase or reduce any differences between the two groups. Extraneous variables cannot be controlled for, and their identification may prove quite difficult. However, the use of organizational measures is helpful in determining whether training has, in fact, enabled volunteers to demonstrate the competencies the training was designed to help them achieve.

The professional trainer of volunteers needs some measure of the effectiveness of training and should select the technique or combination of techniques that is most effective in evaluating the particular training and is consistent with various constraints. Too, it is possible that affective measures provide more information than they are normally given credit for. Often an affective measure is the only one available to the trainer, given organizational and political constraints. Therefore, affective measures should be carefully studied to determine their value relative to cognitive, organizational, and behavioral measures. One comparative study collected affective and cognitive data on 749 participants in a union training program (Confer, 1973). Due to the organizational constraint of privacy, it was not possible to keep the data in such a form that individual cognitive and affective data could be matched. However, the average cognitive and affective scores for each of the ten training sites were calculated; the difference between the mean pre- and posttest scores positively correlated with the mean affective scores ($r = .69$, significant at .05 level; Confer, 1980).

These results suggest the need for further research on the interpretation and use of affective measures in the evaluation of training. If it is found that achievement consistently covaries

with feelings toward the training and that variance in achievement can be predicted from affective measures, then the use of affective measures would take on much greater significance in the evaluation of training. Affective measures are also important in that they may reveal factors responsible for turnover among volunteers.

As mentioned earlier, evaluation can also be used as part of the training itself by using a pretest to make participants aware of the organization's or trainer's expectations and a diagnostic posttest to assist trainers and participants in assessing individuals' training needs. Evaluation can also be used to reinforce the training and new behaviors back on the job. This purpose can be accomplished through a series of follow-up questionnaires. The first follow-up asks if the participants use the skills they learned; the second asks them to describe instances in which they use the skills; and the third asks for the results or evaluation of the efforts undertaken using the particular skills.

Individualizing Training

An ideal training program for volunteers contains components that provide for the fullest possible meshing of individual volunteer's needs with the needs of the volunteer organization. Participants learn best in an environment in which they feel free to learn those things that they believe will benefit themselves and their organization. Thus the trainer must be able to adjust a general training method to the specific needs of the participants and the organization. Interviews and surveys are the most effective devices for individualizing a program for a specific audience. Interview and survey data enable the trainer to select the techniques best suited to the volunteers, the organization, and the skills to be learned. The higher the level of complexity of the skills, the greater the utility of counseling and interviewing in contrast to surveying. Conversely, trainers whose programs involve highly structured and straightforward skills will find surveys and pretests to be most useful in the determination of training techniques.

Similarly, the selection of appropriate training techniques

depends on the nature of the training, the size and diversity of the group to be trained, the felt needs of the volunteers, and the needs identified by the organization. Considerations such as money and politics also affect the selection of training techniques. As noted earlier, the same basic technique (in that case, programmed instruction) can have highly divergent results even though used in organizations that appear similar. Let us review one piece of research that can assist trainers in selecting the appropriate training technique for a particular group of volunteers.

Graves (1966) identifies a series of value systems that operate in our society. Each set of values represents a "level of existence," and each level "is a state of equilibrium through which people pass on the way to other states of equilibrium"; at "a particular level of existence, a person has a psychology which is particular and peculiar to that level" (p. 121). A person's acts, feelings, motivations, ethics, values, and thoughts result in behaviors intended to solve the problems and conflicts associated with a given level. For our purposes, it is most important to note that persons at a particular level tend to prefer particular styles of leadership and training techniques.

Graves identifies seven levels, six of which are relevant to noninstitutionalized adults in contemporary western society:

1. Tribalistic: Persons at this level prefer to stay with their own kind of people, and work for a fair and friendly boss; they follow long-established and traditional ways of doing things.
2. Egocentric: Persons at this level tend to look out for themselves first; they value power and the active exercise of it.
3. Conformist: Persons at this level are bureaucratic; rules, regulations, standards, and instructions guide their behavior.
4. Manipulative: Persons at this level value game playing; prestige, respect, and physical trappings are important to them.
5. Sociocentric: Persons at this level value group activity and belonging.
6. Existential: Persons at this level are spontaneous and free from the constraints that inhibit most others; the challenge of tough goals and the freedom to pursue them are strong motivators.

For each level, we can suggest a training style or set of techniques that is most compatible: (1) tribalistic—sermonizing; (2) egocentric—direct orders and specific instruction; (3) conformist—programming including all details; (4) manipulative—lecture and discussion; (5) sociocentric—group activities; and (6) existential—individualized activities directed toward agreed objectives.

As noted earlier, volunteers are likely to be sociocentric; it appears that a sociocentric value system is more in keeping with the nature of volunteer work. However, the trainer of volunteers should not take the sociocentric nature of volunteers as a given but rather should separately assess each individual and group. Thus, the trainer can adopt techniques most compatible with the value system of the volunteers.

Training should also be adapted to the organization in which the volunteers are to work. Many leaders of volunteer organizations are inclined to assume that their volunteers are fully aware of the organization's goals and needs, that such awareness prompted them to volunteer. Leaders of volunteer organizations, however, tend to shape those organizations to meet their own needs and express their own value systems. As a result, misunderstandings may arise among leaders and groups of volunteers new to the organization.

Organizational goals and needs can be stated in orientation sessions to provide an initial opportunity for new volunteers and established leaders to explore them together. However, orientation sessions are often insufficient to fully integrate new volunteers. Volunteers need more individualized goal identification sessions that provide opportunities for each volunteer to identify congruencies between personal goals and organizational goals. The trainer must establish the environment and processes wherein volunteers in training programs can compare and match their needs, goals, and values to those of the organization.

Individualized training is needed to supplement a group training program because the wide variety of needs and values among volunteers assures that classroom training alone cannot meet all volunteers' needs. Thus the fullest possible use of individualization is almost a necessity. Further, when appropriate, a broad range of community resources can be used to advantage. Local meetings, conventions, and other opportunities seemingly unrelated to training activities can be incorporated into the training program. The opportunity for the volunteer to learn and to grow through volunteer activity can be facilitated through individualization and the identification and legitimization of activities usually unassociated with training. The legitimization of skills and knowledge learned outside the traditional system is sure to benefit the volunteer, the trainer, and the volunteer organization.

In sum, the trainer of volunteers should be concerned with how the participants can best learn as well as what the participants actually learn. Volunteers will learn the skills and knowledge that they perceive as serving their needs, goals, and values. They cannot be forced to learn what they do not want to learn nor what they do not perceive as having relevance to their volunteer activities. It is incumbent upon the trainer of volunteers, therefore, to assist in the thorough exploration of the needs, goals, and values shared by the organization and individual volunteers. The larger that common area, the greater the potential for volunteers' growth through volunteer activity, the more readily volunteers will participate, and the more thorough the integration of volunteers into the volunteer organization.

Ideal Training Program

To demonstrate the elements of an ideal training program for volunteers, it is useful to present an example that is, in small part, hypothetical. But let us first make a basic assumption about the volunteer organization and the volunteers. For situations to which some aspect of this assumption does not apply, the example must be adjusted appropriately. Our assumption is: The volunteers are able to attend an intensive full-time program either because they are not otherwise employed, their employer allows for this time off the job, or the volunteer organization subsidizes participation.

The general objectives of our model training program are

(1) to provide the greatest possible opportunity for participants to identify and learn those skills and knowledge that will be most useful to them as volunteers; (2) to establish an environment wherein participants will be able to test perceived constraints on their ability to perform and to learn; and (3) to reinforce participants' behavioral change from teacher-dependent learners to independent learners.

The first portion of the program is an orientation to the program and establishes the rules and guidelines. More important, some time is spent identifying and examining all individual learning styles and legitimizing individual preferences. Resources available to participants are examined and discussed, including, as appropriate, classroom time, audiotapes and videotapes, books and articles, and community facilities. The trainer explains and demonstrates that all participants are expected to develop performance objectives for their volunteer work and, from those, or from a list of options, to identify instructional objectives. For each appropriate training period, the participants are expected to submit learning contracts specifying the instructional objectives they intend to use (such as formal classroom, written, video, audio, or tutorial) and how they plan to evaluate their accomplishment.

At the end of the orientation, the participants will have analyzed their performance objectives, identified a manageable number of instructional objectives, and submitted their first learning contract to the trainer. A learning contract is simply an agreement between the trainers and an individual participant consisting of five items: (1) the learning objectives to be attained; (2) the activities the participant plans to use to attain each objective; (3) the method for evaluating the attainment of each objective; (4) the assistance, if any, needed from the trainer or the organization to attain each objective; and (5) the length of time for the completion of the contract. In addition, small common-interest support groups will have been formed that will later submit a group project (such as a training program, slide show, or paper) that offers material which the volunteers can directly apply to their volunteer activities.

Following the period of orientation, the trainer should

suggest a selection of short but timely training activities congruent with the individual learning contracts and organizational needs. The selection of topic areas for these sessions should be derived from an examination of the volunteers' performance objectives and learning contracts as well as the organization's objectives. The trainer can be assured that the selected topic areas do indeed fit organizational needs if the correspondences between organizational and individual needs are thoroughly clarified. With appropriate negotiation and counseling, the volunteers' learning contracts will reflect those correspondences. Of course, certain instructional objectives in specific topic areas may be mandatory, independent of the learning contracts. However, the trainer should make explicit the rationale for any mandatory objectives or topics. The trainer should also remind volunteers that it is the attainment of the instructional objectives that is important—not necessarily how they are attained. Tutorials, on-the-job training, attendance at meetings or conventions, and the completion of special projects are all legitimate means for volunteers to attain their learning objectives.

The trainer may wish to explore the possibility of awarding continuing education units for successful completion of instructional objectives. The trainer may be able to develop a relationship with a local university or community college that will result in the awarding of credits for the volunteers' efforts. Too, the American Council on Education has sponsored a project to examine the internal training programs of various organizations and to recommend the awarding of credits should those who complete these programs wish to make such application to a university or a community college in the future. Recognition of this type is important to volunteers as it legitimizes volunteer experience for future job-related efforts. This legitimization of volunteer work is a major concern of the largest group of volunteers, women, as many of them find it necessary to enter the paid labor force.

It is apparent that the role of the trainer in a program such as that just described is critical. In more traditional programs, the bulk of the trainer's effort and time is spent in actual instruction before a group. In the design just described, the

trainer spends considerably more time as a consultant or counselor to the participants. The development of realistic performance objectives, the identification and writing of instructional
objectives, and the preparation of learning contracts are only
part of the additional effort required. The participants also need
some guidance in identifying resources and in overcoming and
discovering barriers to their learning. Some participants may initially resent the trainer's untraditional role. Most traditional
educational experiences are teacher-oriented rather than learner-
oriented, and learners may initially be frustrated or confused by
being held responsible for their learning. That frustration can be
turned to enthusiasm through skilled counseling.

The trainer who attempts to implement an ideal program
will find that the majority of his or her time will be spent in
problem-solving or counseling activities. The focus of these activities should be to assist the organization's leaders and staff in
identifying and solving human resources problems. Under no circumstances should the trainer identify the program and then attempt to identify the problems to which it can be applied.
Rather, the trainer best serves the organization by asking questions before implementing programs requested by leaders. Each
training program should be designed to solve a specific problem
that is, by its nature, solvable by training.

Training advisory committees can help a trainer implement a problem-solving approach. It is standard practice, however, to have a trainer submit schedules of training programs
and outlines of proposed programs to the committee. This procedure should be avoided. The committee should rather examine organizational studies and diagnoses and indexes of human
resources problems. The evaluation data from earlier training
programs should also be available to members of training advisory committees.

Those who serve on training advisory committees may
have training responsibilities in other organizations in which
they are volunteers. Thus, these members' experiences, skills,
and training may well be useful in implementing a problem-solving approach to training. Advisory committee members' needs,
as volunteers, should not be overlooked. Their service on the

committee should provide them with an opportunity to improve their own skills. If committee meetings provide learning opportunities for committee members, such meetings will improve the members' skills, bind the members closer to the organization, and assure that the members consider the necessary data for problem solving in the volunteer organization.

Trainers in volunteer organizations have the opportunity to become recognized as professionals. Their development, the attainment of a full range of skills for human resources development, is critical to this process. Greater opportunities for creative application of these skills are available in volunteer organizations than in any other setting. Trainers in volunteer organizations soon find that the effective development of human resources is not a function of the dollars spent on a development program but rather of the trainer's creativity, intelligence, and abilities.

Summary

Information regarding the human resources of a volunteer organization is the most powerful tool in a trainer's tool kit. Data regarding these resources may be collected during formal and informal discussions with the organization's leaders, staff, and volunteers. Surveys are another source of such information and should be used when appropriate. The examination of organizational performance data often provides clues to human resources problems. Once the data are collected, the trainer should be able to analyze that data and derive hypotheses about the organization's human resources needs. These analyses should be distributed and be used as the basis for further discussion. Evaluation data should also be distributed and shared.

The trainer in a volunteer organization who pursues the recommendations made in this chapter will first concentrate on organizational problems and the needs, goals, and values of the volunteers; then develop training activities that will serve the organization and the volunteers' shared needs; and, finally, use methods of evaluation appropriate to the situation.

Chapter Six

Continuing Education in the Professions

Stanley M. Grabowski

Continuing education in the professions is distinct from pre-service preparation for a profession, although there is a connection between them. Among researchers, however, there is no agreement on what constitutes a profession, despite numerous attempts at definition (Flexner, 1915; DeLancy, 1938; Hughes, 1962; Wilensky, 1964; Vollmer and Mills, 1966; Boyette, Blount, and Petaway, 1971; Schein and Kommers, 1972; Anderson, 1974; Mayhew and Ford, 1974; Rose, 1974; Nyre and Reilly, 1979). In this chapter, *profession* is used in the broadest possible sense to include any occupation designated as a profession by any authoritative source such as investigative researchers, the Bureau of Labor Statistics, and the National Center for Education Statistics. *Continuing education* refers to any and all methods, formal or informal, used for the growth and development of professionals.

There is no question or debate about the need for professionals, in every field, to be involved in some form of continuing education. "For a member of a profession to become and remain learned, he must not only master a substantial body of knowledge developed over a period of years in a customarily long and arduous course of formal study but also must continue learning for the entire period of his professional life" (Cooper, 1974, p. 617). The basic need for continuing education results from the danger of two kinds of obsolescence: rustiness resulting from the lack of proper use of professional knowledge and failure to keep up with new developments. The latter may be attributed to the professional's engaging in repetitive patterns of behavior or to his lacking sensitivity to change (Malmros, 1963). Without continuing education, a professional's half-life may be only six or seven years; that is, within seven years after completing initial professional training and preparation, the professional's competency will decrease by one half if that individual has not undertaken any continuing education.

Other impelling reasons for a professional to continue his education include the need "to establish his mastery of the new conceptions of his own profession," "to grow as a person as well as a professional" (Houle, 1967, pp. 263-264), "to maintain freshness of outlook on the work done," "to retain the power to learn," and "to discharge effectively the social role imposed by membership in a profession" (Houle, 1976, p. 48).

Ideally, professionals will continue to grow and learn as part of their professional commitment, which imposes an obligation to do so. Some professionals, however, respond only to external pressures that have proliferated as the result of public demand that professionals maintain high levels of competence: "This demand has been brought on by certain trends in consumerism. The consumer has become increasingly concerned about the widening gap between what professionals can deliver and what the public expects them to cherish. The perception of this widening gap on the part of the consumer has resulted in a significant loss of public faith and trust in the capability of the current licensure system and of professional organizations to maintain competencies in professional service" (Loring, 1980, p. 12).

Professional schools are hard pressed to include basic knowledge and beginning skills within their limited time allotments for courses, leaving much information and many skills for professionals to acquire and master after completing their formal education. In some professions, the individual is expected to learn some aspects of professional practice after having been admitted to practice. For example, lawyers routinely learn certain skills after admission to the bar, and law schools routinely prescribe continuing education for their graduates. Indeed, there is an assumption and expectation among the leaders of most professions that the need for lifelong learning is so obvious to practitioners that they will pursue it. But the value of lifelong learning is not always communicated systematically by professional schools (Houle, 1980, p. 85). Because professionals' participation in continuing education is partly dependent on their attitude toward education, preprofessional education programs should change their philosophy and structure to encourage professionals to view their education as necessarily continuous rather than terminal (Nakamoto and Verner, 1972, p. 151).

Mandatory continuing education (MCE) for some professionals is already required for membership in some professional organizations, and many states now have laws that require continuing education as a requisite for relicensure. All fifty states specify continuing education as a requirement for one or more professions. While more states are passing laws that extend mandatory continuing education to various professions, MCE is being called into question by individuals, by professional associations, as well by other groups. For example, the Adult Education Association of the U.S.A., at its annual conference in 1979, established a task force on voluntary learning to study MCE. The National Alliance for Voluntary Learning has launched a nationwide campaign against all forms of MCE. Some states are reviewing MCE for the professions because the state sunset laws require a periodic review of all state agencies. In both Colorado and North Dakota, for example, action on continuing education has been suspended (Katz, 1979). The most important criticisms of MCE are that it does not affect performance significantly nor guarantee competence nor screen out incompetent practitioners (Wells, 1977; Mignard, 1978).

In most states, the law requires a professional to attend continuing education offerings or to obtain continuing education units. But such units may be obtained without any testing or evaluation of the learning outcomes. In many professions, practitioners may take courses unrelated to their needs and comply with MCE merely by amassing the required numbers of credit units (Mignard, 1978, p. 21). Laws requiring only that professionals secure units are based on a confusion between attendance and learning. Such laws equate attending a formal educational program or course with education and equate a certificate, diploma, or degree with competence (Illich, 1970). Such laws presume that professionals will never mature sufficiently to become fully independent learners who are self-directed. Ultimately, MCE relinquishes accountability for professionals' learning to the individual and the continuing education program, and perhaps the regulatory force behind MCE (Richards, 1975, p. 260).

Stern, who has championed MCE for professionals, points out how MCE can be abused: "I don't want it done on the cheap. Many professionals coming to us in universities make the simple, breathtaking, corrupt suggestion that the least education they can get away with to satisfy a statutory requirement is what they want. So, for example, dentists go off on a cruise ship to Acapulco, under institutional auspices, if you please, to study orthodontics on the sundeck" (1976, p. 5). However, if MCE were to be implemented as intended, the educational system could not cope with the demand. For example, if there were a nationwide requirement for all professionals to engage in some kind of formal continuing education, there would not be enough providers to deliver it. If the 350,000 physicians in the U.S. were required to take 150 hours of continuing education every three years, as is the case in some states, even double the current number of faculty members in all the medical schools would not be sufficient to deliver the required number of hours.

Legislative requirements to compel professionals to continue their education are not necessary if they are independently seeking ways to improve their performance or willing to innovate new practices. Professionals moving from one aspect of work or setting within their profession to another and professionals returning to practice following a hiatus recognize and readily pursue the learning necessary to gain or regain competency (Houle, 1980, pp. 103-104). The problem of motivating professionals arises most frequently with those whom Houle calls laggards, "those who learn only what they must know if they are to stay in practice. They have built a house without windows and now they live in the dark" (Houle, 1976, p. 50). These individuals generally do not respond to new ideas or do so grudgingly. Mandatory continuing education may compel them to attend educational offerings, but it is questionable whether they will learn anything.

MCE is failing, among other reasons, because the compulsory requirements fail to define competencies and measures for their attainment (Nyre and Reilly, 1979, p. 31). MCE infringes on the time and financial resources of professionals, and forces on them more complex relationships that affect goals as well as motivations. In addition, there remains the question of the effect that MCE has on the self-image and self-direction of professionals (Pennington, 1975, p. 167).

Providers

Continuing education for professionals is made available by numerous providers, and if more legislation is enacted to mandate continuing education, more institutions, agencies, associations, and entrepreneurs will swell the roster of providers. Professional associations have, as one of their overt functions, the continuing education of their members. These associations undertake this function in order to maintain the standards of high quality of services (Pennington, 1975, p. 16). Professional associations ought to be better informed about the needs of their members than any other provider (Loring, 1980), and the more than 12,000 associations in the professions and trades,

with about 10 million members (Eldredge, 1970, p. 27), constitute a tremendous resource for continuing education. Professional associations tend to stress the societal context of professionals' practice, pragmatic issues, and their status in the
sponsorship of continuing education (Knox, 1974, p. 69).

Institutions of higher education, especially through their
professional schools, are actively engaged in continuing education for the professions, partly to exert some leadership and
partly to make money in a highly lucrative market. Programs of
continuing education sponsored by universities tend to use experts and to emphasize knowledge, innovations, and suggestions
regarding how the profession ought to operate (Knox, 1974, p.
69). Institutions of higher education provide continuing education for the professions with academic legitimacy and opportunities for interdisciplinary programs (Loring, 1980, p. 19).

Employing agencies and institutions such as industries
and hospitals are providing in-house continuing education for
professional employees. They are concerned, to a large extent,
with increasing the effectiveness of the professional on the job.

Entrepreneurs and commercial vendors, including publishers, are mounting numerous programs of continuing education for professionals. Whatever their avowed purposes, profit is
one of their goals. Most entrepreneurs have a set program that
they offer in various geographical locations, rarely accommodat-
ing the program to the unique requirements of a specific local-
ity or group. Their presentations tend to be canned and slick.
Some vendors are creating learning packets that they sell to institutions of higher education which, in turn, resell them to professional organizations and individuals (Loring, 1980, p. 17).

Comparative Continuing Education

There is a growing realization among providers of continuing professional education that comparative continuing education in the professions may be the most useful approach to
take in the future. The complexity and interrelatedness of professions compel practioners to rely on various disciplines for
effectiveness in any single profession (Eley, 1970). Surgeons,

engineers, technicians, lawyers, and theologians have a concern for some of the sophisticated procedures used in operating rooms, and all need to share their expertise on this and similar subjects. One report claims that as many as 92 percent of university extension divisions and 50 percent of professional associations have some kind of ongoing cooperative programs in continuing education (Watkins, 1979).

Greater cooperative arrangements among educational institutions, professional associations, and other agencies rendering client services or delivering continuing education for professionals are needed to make competent resources available and accessible. Such an approach not only accommodates the flexibility, diversity, and scope of activities required to meet the needs of practitioners but also recognizes and provides for the interdisciplinary nature of many professions (Conrath, 1970).

Loring suggests that a "collaborative-competitive relationship" needs to be created among various providers (1980, p. 20). Collaboration would ensure the best response to the needs of professionals, while competition would provide sufficient incentives for maintaining high standards and thus ultimately benefit individual professionals engaged in continuing education.

Methods of Delivery

A cursory examination of the brochures and catalogues that announce continuing education for professionals shows that every known method, instructional technique, and device is used by providers, although some professions seem to limit themselves to a few favorite approaches. The list of methods and approaches includes seminars, clinics, workshops, forums, institutes, lectures, demonstrations, colloquia, round-table discussions, audio and video cassettes, telelectures, closed-circuit television, open-circuit television, cable television, radio, computer-assisted instruction, programmed-instruction machines and texts, telephone access, home study programs, lending library resource services, modularized instructional units, experiential learning, films, slides, manuals, books, and traineeships. Continuing education offerings are available for credit as well as not for credit, in formal as well as informal settings, for short or extended terms, as single offerings or as series whether continuous or intermittent.

Much of continuing education is characterized by the transmission of the latest information through various didactic means that only involve the learner passively. Studies show that the influence of such learning on practice is small (Miller, 1963, p. 296). Information is probably not the principal need of practitioners; their need is greater in the area of changing behavior (Wells, 1977). Furthermore, most practitioners are practically oriented and want to learn that which will be useful immediately (Miller, 1963, p. 296).

The issue of continuing education for the professions is further complicated in that some individuals do not use the traditional preparation process to become professionals. Formerly, most aspiring professionals spent considerable time after high school graduation in direct preparation for entering a profession, usually by attending a college, university, or professional school and then completing a period of internship, practice teaching, ward assignment, and other experiences related to qualifying for licenses to practice (Charters, 1970). Now, however, some individuals are entering professions at a period later in life than the usual lock-step progression through school; some are making mid-career changes in professions; and some are developing an avid desire to learn at a time in life later than traditional education permits. Such individuals pursue atypical pre-service and in-service training patterns (Houle, 1980, p. 77).

While providers may be attracting large numbers of professionals to their continuing education offerings, many other professionals are engaged in independent continuing education and learning, without the help of any institutions, agencies, or organizations. Many professionals engage in continuing education through reading journals and books, informal contacts with colleagues, consultations, reading sales literature for new products, and self-directed learning.

Continuing education in the professions must provide for a diversity of approaches inasmuch as many professionals are highly specialized, work in diverse settings, and have specific needs that cannot be met by standardized formats (Houle, 1980, p. 12). Furthermore, "the participation in education essential to improved practice will occur only through good learning experiences" (Nakamoto and Verner, 1972, p. 150).

Continuing education for professionals should emphasize self-education, individualized educational diagnosis, and individualized response rather than instruction and coursework. Continuing education ought to lead practitioners to examine their practices, to identify their educational deficits, and to establish realistic priorities for their educational progress. Practitioners need to be involved in an analysis of their use of available resources (Miller, 1967). Most researchers and writers recommend a self-directed orientation for continuing education for the professions (Knox, 1974, p. 72). The strongest argument in favor of self-directed learning is that individuals are most apt to learn what they have identified as their own educational deficits, and professionals are able to establish realistic priorities for their own learning programs. Houle (1980) used the word *learning* rather than *education* in his title *Continuing Learning in the Professions,* to indicate that the learning individuals and groups accomplish to fulfill their needs and aspirations is more important than the processes and procedures used in formal educational programs.

Finally, continuing education in the professions must be a continuous process. Occasional doses of information or occasional learning experiences do not usually result in meaningful and lasting learning. Learning demands an active effort over a protracted period to allow individuals the opportunity to absorb information or to bring an experience to bear upon their knowledge and skills so that they can apply and evaluate the new information. Education and learning require more than exposure; they also require an engagement with reality (Dill, 1972, p. 54).

Summary

Continuing education for the professions is now an integral part of professional life, even though the best ways to encourage and facilitate it are still subjects of controversy. The need for updating and further development by professionals will escalate as consumers continue to demand greater efficiency and proficiency from professionals. Mandatory continuing education does not seem to be the means to protect consumers' interests. Ideally, of course, professionals ought to be so dedicated and committed to their profession that they continue their education in any one of several ways. Apparently many professionals do continue their education as self-directed learners, and perhaps that is the best way to proceed.

Providers mounting continuing education offerings for professionals should consider the following recommendations. First, programs should be based and integrated within the practice of the professional, ideally at the place where most problems occur. Second, programs should meet the felt needs of practitioners. Third, the content and procedures of continuing education should be based on a systematic needs assessment of practitioners' deficiencies in knowledge and skills and their undesirable attitudes as reflected in their performance. Fourth, continuing education should be professionally controlled (Schmidt, 1968). Fifth, the complexity of the various professions and their interdependence call for a more intensely interdisciplinary approach to continuing education in the various professions.

Chapter Seven

Training
in Organizations

Irwin R. Jahns

Training is a bane for some, salvation for others, but for most it is misunderstood and misused. Many educators identify training with the process used to teach dogs to sit, roll over, and retrieve. Others acknowledge it to be within the spectrum of teaching and learning but are uncertain as to its place therein. In the world of work and economic enterprise, some view training as an expensive luxury to be tolerated only under duress or to convey a facade of accomplishment. Very few recognize the importance of training to the attainment of desired organizational ends.

Unfortunately, similar misunderstandings persist among those who study and practice adult education. Although they acknowledge training to be part of the field of adult education,

94

they do not always perceive it as an entirely respectable endeavor. In the minds of many, training differs from other forms of adult education in that it is imposed on unwilling subjects who have little choice in the matter. The compulsory nature of training, they argue, contradicts the central premise of adult education as a voluntary enterprise. Other adult educators perceive training as distinct from education because they view the participant as relegated to the mere status of a responding organism, whereas education requires the learner to be an active collaborator. To these educators, the word *training* suggests that people are trained in the same way that animals are trained, that training requires minimal or no intellectual activity. Indeed, the school of scientific management reportedly was based, in part, on the assumption that thinking by workers is detrimental to efficiency; thinking is to be done by management, removed from the immediate work environment.

Other reasons can be advanced to explain the negative image of training. Adult education is voluntary, training is not. In adult education, the learner is perceived as a holistic entity, at least in theory, whereas training focuses on only one aspect of the individual. The purpose of adult education is to facilitate the maturation, growth, and development of the learner. It is concerned with "the process by which men and women . . . seek to improve themselves" or "any process by which individuals, groups or institutions try to help men and women improve" (Houle, 1972, p. 32). Training, in contrast, is viewed as being concerned with shaping individuals to conform to the dictates of the employing organization. The trainees are perceived as robots whose behavior must be controlled and shaped.

Knowles (1970) is careful to minimize his use of the word *training* when discussing the mission of the adult educator. He posits this mission as the satisfying of the needs and goals of individuals, institutions, and society. That institutions have legitimate needs and goals that must be met is often overlooked by adult educators. The development of public understanding and support and the improvement of institutional operations are among these. Knowles also identifies institutions' need for "the development of individuals in the institution's constituency in the direction of the institution's goals for them" (p. 30). The training of individuals to meet the needs of institutions is not, as some claim, antithetical to meeting the needs and goals of individuals and of society because institutions' needs can be met through humanistic procedures that respect and indeed further individuals' and society's goals.

Distinctions between adult education and training are also observed by institutions that have one staff responsible for the design and implementation of a public adult education program and another staff responsible for training. The training personnel, often located in organizational units separate from adult education, are defined as participating not in adult education but rather in the in-service training of institutional employees. Their functions are directed to system employees, whereas adult education efforts are directed toward constituents external to the system. This bifurcation reinforces the seeming separation and distinction between adult education and training.

As one considers other current and past practices in education, additional evidence of a negative orientation toward training becomes evident. At one time it was accepted practice to speak of *teacher training* and *nurses training*; these are now referred to as *teacher education* and *nursing education*. *In-service training* has been replaced by *in-service education, continuing education, staff development,* or *professional development. Leadership training* has become *leadership development. Physical education* has replaced *physical training. Management training* has become *management development.* In only a few areas is the term *training* now acceptable: on the football field, in the boxing ring, and in the military. Too, *on-the-job training* and *volunteer training* are still acceptable; but newly employed workers need to be *oriented* to their jobs, managers need to be *developed,* and professionals need *continuing education.*

Even though the term *training* is not entirely respectable in many institutional settings, neither is *education* in other contexts. *Management education* can take place in a school of business, but *management development* occurs in industry. *Continuing professional education* is provided by university extension and continuing education divisions, but *professional development* occurs in an agency. *Vocational preservice education* is provided in a vocational-technical school, but *staff development* and *job improvement* occur in the workplace.

If some see training as limited and limiting, others see education as irrelevant and superfluous to the task at hand. If some consider adult education a difficult concept to describe and define (Schroeder, 1970, pp. 27-29), the concept of training has proved itself to be just as elusive. Yet both are concerned with the design and delivery of instruction and with the facilitation of learning.

In this chapter, we present a synthesis of the central tendencies involved in such concepts as training, education, staff development, and organizational development. From this perspective a functional notion of training will emerge. Our discussion of the training process focuses on its role in organizational systems and its function as a mechanism for organizational stability and change. We conclude this chapter by posing some fundamental questions to be considered in analyzing and integrating various systems of training.

Training—Its Relationship to Education

Training is concerned with the role performance of workers in organizational systems. More precisely, it is concerned with the development and maintenance of competencies to perform specific roles by persons holding positions in existing systems. In comparison, education is concerned with the more general growth and development of an individual (Lynton and Pareek, 1967, pp. 5-7). However, training cannot be strictly differentiated from education: The processes of learning involved in each are similar, as are the methods and techniques used in their implementation. Thus training and education are related, although the former focuses on the performance of predetermined tasks and the latter on personal maturation and growth.

Lynton and Pareek describe education as primarily concerned with the acquisition of knowledge about something, whereas training is concerned with the development of skill in doing something. But both the acquisition of knowledge and the acquisition of skill, Lynton and Pareek note, require understanding and the motivation to apply the knowledge or skill acquired. Thus, although education and training differ in the conceptual and performance competencies they require, they do demand certain efforts that are similar.

An approach that further clarifies the difference between education and training is the examination of the ends or goals that providers and participants in learning activities seek to attain. If the participant's goal is to improve role performance in a position held in a specific organizational system, and the provider's goal is to help the participant, by whatever means, to improve himself in relation to that position, they are both engaged in training. If the participant seeks preparation for generalized role performance, positions, or organizational settings or engages in learning activities for the purpose of self-fulfillment, and the provider facilitates these goals, they are engaged in education.

Thus among the participants in any specific learning activity, some could be seeking education, others training. For example, consider the participants in a ten-week course on the care and propagation of cacti and other succulent plants. Some participants might be seeking to improve their skills as operators of specialist greenhouses, others to fulfill their personal and amateur interest in plants. Similarly, a university course in staff training and development may attract regularly enrolled students, who take the course for academic credit toward their degree, and part-time students currently employed by state agencies, voluntary associations, and school systems, who seek to improve their performance in their specific roles as employees. Although the content of the course is similar for all participants and the intention of the university is to offer education, for some participants the course is a training experience.

Training, then, is that part of the professional field of adult education whose central focus is the role performance of persons in organizational systems. Training contributes to the life-long growth and development of people in its emphasis on the adequate performance of specific roles in agencies, organizations, and institutions. In sum, training encompasses those acts, events, and episodes in which people engage to improve their performance in specific job-related tasks. The factor that differentiates training from education is the specificity of the position, the person, and the work setting. Education prepares people for relatively undifferentiated roles, positions, and work settings; training is concerned with an individual's performance in a specific position at a given work setting.

Responsibility for Training

With this generic perspective of training, we now briefly explore two critical areas: first, the responsibility for role performance on the job and, second, the responsibility for training. Unfortunately, trainers often erroneously assume that they have major responsibility for the role performance of workers in their jobs. But responsibility for such performance lies with the person in the job position and his supervisor, not with the trainer. The individual and supervisor are responsible for the quality and quantity of performance in any given position, and the supervisor of the supervisor is also responsible for the performance of the person who is supervised, and so on through the organizational hierarchy. This premise is as true in the upper echelons of management as it is in the lowest levels of the organization's structure.

Those who have responsibility for role performance in specific positions are greatly assisted by organizational procedures that facilitate the recruitment, screening, and placement of persons who already possess the necessary competencies. When these procedures are successful, qualified people who can effectively contribute to the organization's functions are incorporated into the system. But seldom can an organization hire people who already possess all the required competencies. Thus the organization must assume the responsibility for ensuring that newly employed persons acquire needed competencies and develop new skills as need for them arises.

Supervisors are first expected to orient each employee not only to the organization and its purpose but also to his place in the organization and the specific expectations and role performance associated with that position. The supervisor then, in addition to other tasks at whatever level, also performs a training function. Often simple job instruction, monitoring of work performance, and providing feedback to the employee are adequate. Some organizations designate specific persons or a staff department to provide supervisors with supportive services for training, staff development, and the like. But these individuals merely provide assistance and support to the supervisors; they do not assume responsibility for role performance.

Responsibility for training cannot be as easily placed as responsibility for role performance. Clearly, the goal of training is to improve trainees' performance, and the trainer is responsible for the outcomes of the training effort. But is the trainer solely responsible for training? To answer this question, one must sort out responsibility for the conduct of training from responsibility for the process of training. At the risk of oversimplification, we can state that supervisors and managers, those responsible for role performance, are responsible for specifying those performances they want modified, instilled, or changed through training. These become the ends or goals toward which training is directed. This specification of performance is not the responsibility of the trainers. Their task is to design and manage learning opportunities that efficiently and effectively attain the ends and goals specified by management. Trainers may assist supervisors in establishing the ends and goals of training, but in this they merely provide support to supervisors. Thus responsibility for training is shared by trainers, participants, and the work organization (Lynton and Pareek, 1967, p. 10).

Related to the issue of responsibility for training is the ambiguity of the locus of the training function. Training is conducted by many persons in organizational systems. It may be a full-time, officially designated responsibility for some; for others it is a part-time function closely linked to other position responsibilities. Treffman (1978) portrays eight phases in the evolvement of training in organizations. At the most elementary level, the individual employee directs or selects his own learning experiences. These might be mere experimentation with a variety of ways of carrying out the job or may include interaction with others, including external agents, that lead to modifications of role performance. During the second phase, the supervisor becomes the principal training agent. Throughout succeeding phases, work associates become the primary training agents, and an assistant supervisor, or an assistant to the supervisor, might have part-time responsibility for training. During these initial phases, training is a relatively undifferentiated process in the organization. Training takes place in the work unit and is closely associated with other functions performed in that unit.

As training continues to evolve as a formalized system in the organization, a division of official responsibility may emerge. Members of a department or unit in the organization may be assigned responsibility for training in that unit, and some individuals may be assigned or may assume part-time training responsibilities for the overall organization. Their responsibilities may include orientation of new members to the organization and coordination of training being conducted in separate units within the organization. The staff may also expand the coverage of training to involve all of the members of the organization.

As the organization grows in size and complexity, it may develop a separate staff department whose central function is the coordination of existing training within the work units and the provision of training not offered by existing work units. This training system may continue to evolve from a separate staff department into a semiautonomous educational institution associated with the parent organization but with responsibilities beyond the provision of training and service to its parent system.

Thus, as an organization's training program evolves, new forms of training are introduced that are more formal and differentiated, and these forms supplement earlier phases. The early forms continue to be used, and the newer forms facilitate those forms of training and deal with training needs that extend across and are common to many work units within the organization. The more developed forms function primarily to facilitate, coordinate, and augment, rather than replace, training within the work units.

Unfortunately, Treffman's scheme does not consider or-

ganizations' use of external training. The use of external resources is an integral component of an organization's training
program. Quite often in-house trainers do not actually conduct
training but provide supportive services and coordination for
training conducted by others within the organization. Often
trainers must locate external training resources and consultants
to assist in the design and conduct of needed training. Lauffer
(1977, pp. 3-15) identifies several external resources available to
organizational systems: universities and professional schools,
professional associations, various public and private agencies
and coordinating bodies, independent entrepreneurs, and groups
and organizations in private practice. An organization may hire
consultants on a part-time or on-call basis, and these consultants
become, in effect, temporary members of the organizational
system. Or the organization may sponsor its regular members'
attendance at training programs conducted outside the work
setting.

In sum, trainers in an organizational system contribute to
the training process, but they are not responsible for the entire
process. Training is an organizational function to which many
individuals contribute.

Training and Organizational Change

How then does the training process function in the overall organization? What is its relationship to other organizational
processes? All organizations seek to efficiently and effectively
accomplish goals. (The setting of these goals is a complex
topic that is beyond the scope of this chapter. For a discussion
of how organizations develop goals, see Thompson and McEwen,
1960; Beder, 1978.) In attempting to achieve their goals, all organizations must establish processes and procedures instrumental to desired ends and contributive to goal attainment. An organization must recruit, select, and place personnel who can
contribute in some meaningful way. Each of the organization's
units, in turn, contributes in some way to goal attainment.

Although recruitment, selection, and placement are not
normally considered central to training, they are critical in con-

tributing to effective individual and organizational performance. These processes provide the human resources upon which the organization depends for the accomplishment of its goals. To the extent that these processes are effective, the need for training is minimal; but, if these processes are ineffective, training is required. In this sense, training is one of several social control mechanisms in an organization. One of its primary functions is to socialize individuals into the organization and to help them develop appropriate expectations for role performance in their specific positions. By helping employees to better respond to the organization's needs, training contributes to organizational stability.

Training has a broader purpose, however. It is also concerned with staff development, that is, with facilitating the continuing growth and development of individuals as contributors to the organization. Staff development intends not merely to help individuals perform in specific positions but also to maximize the career potential of individuals as contributors to the organizational system. The goal of staff development is to help individuals realize their full potential rather than merely to best fulfill the role expectations of their current position.

Staff development usually requires a variety of training experiences, patterned in a way that affords individuals the opportunity to develop a broader understanding and knowledge of the organization and its various processes, and more importantly, of their own capabilities and potentials as individuals within the organization. Individuals are provided the opportunity to experience the functioning of a number of work units within the organization, usually through some planned sequence of job rotation. Job rotation allows individuals to learn and practice a variety of skills and to work in a variety of organizational situations under the tutelage of experienced supervisors. Staff development may also include opportunities for study in other organizations, participation in seminars and workshops provided by independent training firms and academic institutions, attendance at professional conferences, and the like. A systematic program of such opportunities allows employees to maximize their growth and development as contributors to the organization.

Staff development may be formalized and instituted by the employing organization as part of its overall training and personnel development effort. Too, individual employees may systematically plan their own development program for purposes congruent with organizational needs or with their own aspirations for personal and career growth and development. To the extent an organization institutes and maintains human resources development programs, it assures itself of a steady supply of increasingly competent individuals to fill positions in its structure. Organizations that do not have such programs are forced to rely on their ability to recruit competent persons from other organizations and institutions.

Staff or human resources development is a training function that can be performed within the organization. It is not necessarily performed by the person or unit formally designated as responsible for training. The coordination of staff development activities and the facilitation for engagement in such activities may be assigned to managers throughout the organization or to staff units such as the personnel or the training unit. In any case, the training unit can contribute substantially to staff development.

A third function that training can perform in the organization is broader and more complex than either the training of individuals for specific positions or the provision of opportunities for staff growth and development. Training can contribute to organizational development if training is firmly established as a key element in organizational decision and action processes. Let us briefly outline how organizations develop and change, in order to understand how training can contribute to the articulation of new goals, policies, and procedures. Figure 1 illustrates the basic steps in organizational development.

Within every organization, some dissatisfaction exists with the present state of affairs, or some preference exists for a more desirable state of affairs. The dissatisfaction or desired change may concern the function of the entire organization or of a subunit of the organization. Various forces external or internal to an organization may generate the felt need for change. Examples of external forces include changes in government

Figure 1. The Training Process in Organizational Systems

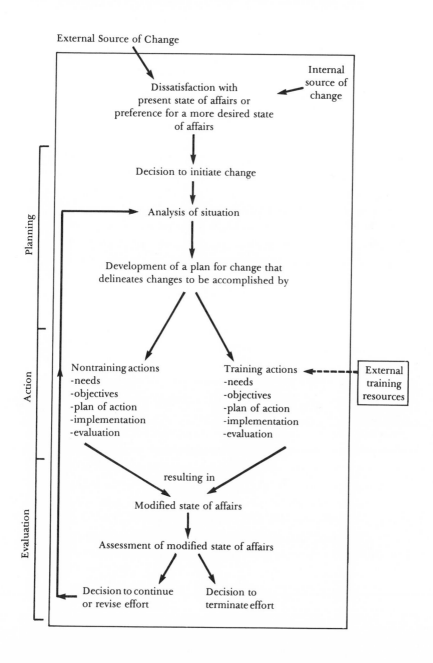

regulations, recent court actions, depleted markets, competition from other organizations, changing client populations, shifting resources, and the like; internal forces include level of morale, production levels, interdepartmental coordination, employee turnover, wastage, and the like. In addition to these negative forces that compel change, new opportunities, such as new markets, new technologies, improved procedures, and more efficient work methods, require change within organizations.

The mere existence of dissatisfaction or of desired preferences, however, is seldom sufficient to generate action for change. For an organization to effect change, management must have the motivation, desire, and commitment to engage necessary resources. Havelock (1973) presents one model of the process by which dissatisfaction results in change:

1. initial disturbance (pressure from inside or outside, crisis)
2. feeling of need and decision to do "something" about the need
3. diagnosis of the need as a problem
4. search for solutions
5. application of a possible solution to the need
6. satisfaction (problem is solved) or dissatisfaction (process must begin anew)

This process may be more or less consciously followed and rational procedures more or less incorporated into this process. A conscientious, rational diagnosis of needs is useful in precluding premature or inadequate definitions of the problem, definitions which could result in the adequate or inappropriate selection of solutions. Leavitt (cited by Barnes, 1969) suggests that problem diagnosis include consideration of tasks, people, technology, and organizational structure.

The result of the search for solutions should be a more or less rationally developed, more or less explicit plan of action. This plan of action should specify the problem, the goals of change, resources to be committed to the effort, the people to be involved, the actions that are needed to achieve the goals, the schedule for these actions, and the procedures for assessing whether the goals have been adequately achieved. The plan should distinguish those actions that require training from those that do not. The plan should detail procedures for coordinating, sequencing, and implementing both the training actions and the nontraining actions.

From such a well-developed plan, persons responsible for designing and conducting the training and the nontraining actions can engage in detailed planning that takes into account the specific needs, objectives, activities, and evaluation procedures relevant to their area. After they implement their plans, they can assess whether the specific objectives have been realized. If planning, coordination, and scheduling are well executed, the training and nontraining plans should result in the organization's progress toward its goals for change. Success toward those goals may lead to termination of a particular plan. Lack of progress may be addressed by a decision to continue the planned effort or to modify it.

In this coordinated sequence of events, training is not assumed to be sufficient to produce desired organizational changes. It must be accompanied by nontraining activities that enhance, support, and utilize the changes brought about through training. If the competencies employees gained through training are to be transferred to the workplace, then the entire organizational system must support that effort. For example, consider the case of teachers who attend training workshops designed to develop their skills in new instructional techniques. Often teachers return from training to face apathetic superiors, hostile peers, and materials inadequate to implement their newly acquired skills. If the school is unwilling to make concomitant changes, the teacher's training will not result in changes within the school system. The training of individuals, in isolation from other organizational efforts, is seldom sufficient to bring about significant changes in the system.

The organizational model shown in Figure 1 suggests another consideration related to the transfer to the work setting of the competencies acquired during training. As we just noted, one factor that affects transfer is the implementation of necessary supporting nontraining activities. Another is the appropriateness of the goals for training established in the organizational plan. If those goals were unrealistic or ill conceived, training that makes a significant contribution to reaching those goals may have little effect on organizational behavior. Trainers often face the problem of whether to proceed to establish training objectives and plans of action if the goals they have been given by the organization are unclear. Lynton and Pareek (1967) caution trainers against proceeding if the organization's goals are unclear. Trainers cannot and should not attempt to establish or clarify goals for the organization. They should, rather, discuss the problem with those who wrote the goals.

Trainers can be held accountable only for the successful attainment of the training goals presented in the organizational plan. Similarly, directors of nontraining activities, planners, and organizational decision makers can be held accountable only for their respective roles in the plan.

In the development of an organizational plan, designers must consider trainers' role in the overall process of organizational change. Are trainers to be considered merely in the employment of organizational decision makers and responsive to the directives given them? Or are they expected to be fully involved participants who work collaboratively with decision makers and planners? Likewise, are formally designated trainers to be responsible for initiating proposals for organizational change? To what extent are they to be involved in organizational assessments of need and in delineating those changes that can most appropriately be addressed by training?

Both the plan's designers and trainers should determine the nature and extent to which external training resources are required for the successful implementation of the plan. Many organizational systems have limited internal capability to provide adequate training; consequently, they are dependent on external resources. A plan for change requires designers and trainers to decide how necessary external resources are to be engaged and who is to be responsible for identifying and obtaining these resources. Decisions on these issues have a significant effect on the contributions that training can make to organizational stability or change.

In summary, we have considered three functions that training serves: to help individuals improve their performance in their positions, to help individuals realize their potential for growth and development, and to contribute to organizational change. Each of these approaches to training has a particular goal and affects the organization in a particular way. However, in the final analysis, all training is concerned with the role performance of persons occupying positions in organizational systems. Training, as we have seen, is inextricably intertwined with other organizational processes, and responsibility for training as an organizational process is shared by many, including trainers, participants, and decision makers. Trainers can be held responsible only for role performance that meets the expectations attached to their positions in the organization; judgment regarding the need for training, the nature of the training, and the utilization of training rests with the organization.

Delivery of Training

One might conclude from the foregoing discussion that there is a single model for trainers to follow. The general field of adult education quite often explicitly or implicitly suggests such a model. Knowles (1970), for example, consistently advocates an andragogical approach in which there is a high degree of collaborative interchange among all participants involved in the design and conduct of learning activities. This approach may be contrasted with the pedagogical approach, a pattern in which professionals assume responsibility for design and delivery, and learners merely engage in that which is offered. But andragogy and pedagogy are not the only alternatives for organization's training systems. A training system's design and delivery depend on its relationship to the organization and the organization's expectations.

To respond to organizational goals, training systems use a variety of approaches in designing and delivering training. Five general approaches can be discerned, each of which is characterized by a certain division of responsibility between trainers and organizations, and by different assumptions about the expectations for role performance throughout the training process.

First, there is the approach that has been called the menu model. In this approach, training systems offer a menu of pre-packaged training activities, events, and products that can be purchased by organizations. The preparation and content of these items are the responsibility of the training system. Their design may be the result of careful analysis and study of potential market needs, or the consequence of fad, tradition, previous consumer demand, and the like. The organization, as a potential purchaser, has the responsibility for deciding what it wants and needs, and for selecting those items it purchases. The contact between the training system and the organization consists of the exchange of the prepackaged item for its purchase cost. The training system creates those items that it believes are market-able, and it must often engage in elaborate promotion proce-dures to enhance sales. The organizational system must exercise judgment regarding the reliability and utility of the items it pur-chases and of the credibility of claims set forth by the seller. As in any sales transaction, the buyer must beware.

A second approach can be designated a special-order model. The training system offers its technical capability to de-sign training activities, events, and products that will meet the specifications of the organization. The organization thus is re-sponsible for deciding what it wants and for setting forth the exact specifications to which the special order must conform. The training system is responsible for delivering a completed product to the specifications of the organizational system. It does not question those specifications, nor is it concerned with the efficacy of the order or the use for which the training ma-terials are intended.

A third approach is the diagnostic model. In this ap-proach, the training system offers the organization its compe-tency to diagnose training needs and to prescribe appropriate courses of action. The organization has the responsibility for recognizing the existence of some dissatisfaction or preference but need not pinpoint its nature or source. The organization se-lects a training system in which it has confidence and contracts for that system's diagnostic and prescriptive services. The or-ganization must satisfy the training system's requests for information needed for the diagnostic process. The training system, in turn, is expected to provide objective diagnosis and appropriate prescriptions for the organization. The training system's responsibility ends upon delivery of the prescription, often in the form of an elaborate report. The organization has full responsibility for accepting and implementing the prescription. In contrast to the menu model or the special-order model, the diagnostic model is characterized by a greater interchange between the organization and the training system in the determination of training needs and alternative courses of action.

The fourth approach is characterized by an even greater interchange of efforts between the organization and the training system. In this collaborative model, the two systems are jointly engaged in assessing needs, diagnosing the organizational situation, exploring alternative courses of action, selecting and implementing a plan, and evaluating the consequences. The training system offers its competence to work jointly with the organization and has responsibility for employing its unique capabilities as a more-or-less integral part of the organization. The organization has responsibility for openness and commitment to this collaborative effort. The primary intention of this approach is to solve a problem, remove a dissatisfaction, or attain a preferred state of affairs. A secondary intention is for the organization to enhance its own abilities to independently conduct future efforts. "Learn by doing" is an oft-cited motto of this approach, but the doing takes precedence over the learning.

The fifth approach to training practice, the organizational learning model, is similar to the fourth, but with one major distinction. The primary intention of either or both the organization and the training system is for the former to increase its ability to engage in the training process independent of external guidance, direction, or control. The resolution of any given training need or problem is secondary to the organization's goal of attaining self-sufficiency in problem solving. The relationship between the organization and the training system is characterized by mutually derived, collaborative efforts to maximize the organization's capabilities to undertake future efforts with decreasing dependence on outside resources. The training system has the primary responsibility for helping the organization learn, that is, develop its knowledge of, understanding about, and skill in engaging in the training process. The organization is responsible for its commitment to efforts to increase its self-help abilities. In contrast to the collaborative model, doing is not directly a means for learning, but learning is a means for developing the abilities to do.

The selection of any one of these five approaches results in different consequences to the organization. For example, the approach determines the organization's relative dependence on a training system in the provision of available activities, events, and products to be used in training. Each organization develops expectations about what a training systems is to offer and what the organization is prepared to offer in return. Should these expectations deviate from other organizational practices or counter the best interests of the organization or the training system, the resulting training program may prove ineffective in contributing to organizational goals of stability or change.

Summary

We have posited training to be a subfield of adult education. The primary concern of training is the development and maintenance of individuals' competence to perform in specific roles in their positions in organizations. In its pure form education is concerned with knowledge about something, whereas training is concerned with performance in doing something; but the overlap between these goals is significant. One means for differentiating between the two is to examine the intention of the participants.

Responsibility for training within an organization is shared by trainers, supervisors, and management. Training serves to help individuals fulfill the role expectations of their present positions in the organization, contributes to the growth and development of individuals and their future potential as organization members, and contributes to the organization's development. The relationship between the organization and its training system, whether internal or external, may follow a menu model, a special-order model, a diagnostic model, a collaborative model, or an organizational learning model.

These observations generate seven fundamental questions that can be departure points for detailed analysis of a given organization's training program:

1. To what extent are provisions made for preparing trainees for generalized roles, positions, and organizational systems as compared to specific role performances associated with specific positions in specific organizational systems?
2. Is the organizational system or the training subsystem assuming responsibility for adequate role performance on the job?
3. Who is assuming responsibility for training? What kinds of contributions to the design and delivery of training are made by the organization and the training system?
4. What are the implicit and explicit ends or goals of the training that is provided? Does the training seek to help trainees fill designated positions, to enhance the growth and development of trainees as part of an overall plan for individual and staff development, or to facilitate the attainment of desired organizational changes?
5. Is the training conceptualized as an integral part of other organizational processes or as separate from and independent of these processes? To what extent are internal and external resources utilized?
6. Does the training system serve to generate the need for change on the part of the organization or does it merely respond to the organization's requests and directives?
7. What is the character and state of the exchange relationship between the organization and its training system? Is it characterized by a single approach to the delivery of training or by multiple approaches?

Training is a special variety of adult education arising from the legitimate needs and goals of institutions. Training officers, through their judicious employment of appropriate training approaches, play a major role in managing and regulating organizational stability and change. And, as the chapter has shown, they can serve institutional needs and goals through humanistic educational procedures that also respect and further individuals' and society's goals.

Chapter Eight

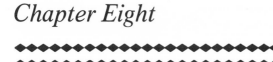

Training in Business and Industry

Stephen P. Becker

The use of training in business and industry is growing dramatically. The reasons for this growth include a highly inflationary economy that increases the cost of labor, the increasing number of government regulations regarding personnel policies and equal opportunity, rapidly changing technology that requires continuing education, and the increasing population of training and development professionals formally trained in behavioral sciences and instructional technology.

At one time training was considered little more than common sense. Managers would identify an individual who was performing in an outstanding way in a particular job and assign that individual to train another person. That approach to training is still used, but many managers now realize that significant productivity can be gained through more formalized employee development systems and procedures. Most training can be categorized by one of six general classifications: organizational development, management and executive development, supervisory development, sales training, technical-professional training, and skills training. Let us examine each of these in turn.

Organizational development (OD) is concerned with change in a large system. Typically, the OD professional works on organizational issues that are concerned with interpersonal relationships, organizational structure, organizational consequences (including reward and punishment systems), management style and policy, as well as other processes that affect the work environment within an organization. The aim of OD is to minimize conflicts within the organization so that the tasks and mission of the organization can be achieved more productively.

OD professionals typically apply a standard four-step procedure. First, they establish a contract with a significantly powerful person or group of people in the organization. Second, they specify a strategy or tactic for creating change. Third, they implement that strategy. Fourth, they evaluate the results of their effort. Strategies for change include team building, third-party consultation, surveys of organizational climate, the establishment of performance appraisal systems, organizational restructuring, conflict-reduction programs, the creation of incentive systems, and the development of training programs.

Generally, OD specialists, more than other training professionals, are concerned with employees' emotions and feelings at work. Their concern with the quality of work life in large organizations leads them to look not only at individual people and small groups but also at the work itself. This perspective may lead them to suggest various strategies for job enrichment. Whatever strategy they choose, OD professionals are concerned with improving the achievement of the organization as a whole rather than attempting to increase the performance of specific individuals. This view of organizational life tends to make OD training the most difficult kind of training undertaken by an organization. Strategies frequently have long-term effects and require a long time to develop and implement.

OD professionals tend to be the most highly paid individuals within the training profession and to have the highest level of formal education. In major corporations, many OD specialists have a doctorate and a great number have a master's degree. Those who aspire to become trainers usually take a master's degree in business administration with a concentration in organizational behavior and then assume a professional role within industry. OD professionals have created a national organization, the OD Network, that has more than 10,000 members. In addition, the American Society for Training and Development (ASTD) has an OD division, the society's largest division, that had approximately 3,000 members in 1980.

The second large category of training is management and executive development. There are few subjects that chief executive officers like to discuss more than the development of their junior executives. Management and executive development typically takes the form of seminars and workshops intended to increase the knowledge and skills of junior executives. These workshops and seminars may last from one to ten days and cover functional topics ranging from finance and marketing to subjects as sophisticated as strategic planning and managing creativity. These seminars and workshops are not viewed as part of managers' formal education even though participation may be required by the organization. They are viewed as continuing education, intended to improve managers and enhance their present competency within their current position or to prepare them for higher-level opportunities.

In addition to seminars and workshops sponsored by companies, many universities and graduate schools of business sponsor executive development programs. Many organizations routinely send key managers to one of these programs, which may last from two weeks to an entire year. Typically, the company schedules an individual for a program one to two years in advance and pays the entire cost of tuition, living expenses, and salary during the time the manager is in attendance. Management development also occurs through job rotation and planned exposure to new kinds of management activities such as project teams or management committees.

The third category of training is supervisory development. Supervisory development typically consists of short-term workshops or training programs for skills that can be applied on the job immediately at the conclusion of the program. Courses cover such topics as time management, decision making, leadership skills, managing by objectives, effective interviewing, and production scheduling. The topics of supervisory workshops tend to be less conceptual than those offered in management development seminars. In addition, supervisors do not have as much opportunity for job rotation as middle- and upper-level managers. Companies are also generally reluctant to send lower-level supervisors to any outside programs. Most of their training takes place within the organization that employs them.

Sales training tends to be a subspecialty within the total context of training and development. Trainers who specialize in sales training typically do not later develop other kinds of training specialties such as management development or organizational development; and trainers in other specialties typically do not add sales training to their career repertoire. Sales training is like supervisory training in that it tends to incorporate many short-term, skills-oriented programs.

Technical-professional training is for people who want to enter specific jobs, such as computer operators, electronics technicians, executive assistants, or photographic chemists. The training programs involve substantial classwork and last from six weeks to a year or longer. Technical-professional training tends to stress the acquisition of knowledge and skills and their application.

Skills training is often required of nonmanagerial employees, including assemblers, machine operators, or receptionists. Such jobs require certain skills that are not particularly difficult to master and can be learned on the job with very little formal instruction. Frequently, the trainer is a coworker or an immediate supervisor rather than a professional in the field of training.

Forms of Training

Training generally takes two forms. The first is institutionalized training, that is, training that has been in place for an extended time. Because individuals need to learn certain skills and functions in order to survive within the organization, the organization has many employees enter a training system of standardized programs. This kind of training is necessary for orientation, for learning company policies, for mastering product knowledge, or for gaining other knowledge and skills required by many jobs within the organization. These standardized training programs are run on a continuing basis.

The second form training takes is training in problem solving. It is in this area that training is making its greatest contributions and gaining credibility within corporate settings (Laird, 1978). Professional trainers find that they can have ready access to key managers in an organization and make significant contributions to the profitability and productivity of an organization if they address an organization's goals and its specific problems in achieving those goals. Business organizations are not organized to educate people but rather to earn profits for their stockholders.

Thus the present trend in training and development is to consider organizational problems and analyze organizational performance to determine whether training is a solution or partial solution to the problems (Becker, 1978). Trainers know that problems have many causes, some of which are behavioral and some of which are not. If analysis reveals that a problem is caused by the behavior of individuals, then training may in fact be a solution. The trainer seeks to determine whether training can help the organization achieve its business goals and objectives rather than simply trying to sell educational programs to managers who may not see the need for such programs. This businesslike approach is giving industrial education a reputation of practicality and efficiency.

The Training Process

Regardless of the type of training, the training process follows a pattern of ten steps.

The first step is an analysis of the organization's performance. The importance of such performance analysis was brought to the attention of trainers in 1970 with the work of

Mager and Pipe (1970), Harless (1970), and the Praxis Corporation (1970). The focus of prior work had been the performance discrepancies of individuals rather than those of large organizations. One theme of the newer approach is that a great deal of analysis should be done before any training program is constructed. A second theme is that there are a variety of solutions other than training for solving performance problems. Such alternatives include altering reward and punishment systems, creating feedback systems for employees' self-evaluation of performance, and removing interference or obstacles from the workplace so that tasks can be accomplished more readily. The identification of these kinds of behavioral solutions is a very important contribution to the training field. As more trainers learn how to analyze performance problems, training programs become more productive.

The second step in the training process is the creation of an integrated plan. Training alone cannot solve a major organizational problem; rather, training must be integrated with other business decisions to yield a complete solution to the problem or to achieve a goal.

Third, once it has been determined that training for a given job is required to solve a problem or to realize an opportunity, a competency description must be developed. A competency description states the human qualities required for superior performance within a job. This research step helps to ensure that the correct learning objectives will be used as the basis for the training program.

Fourth, the learning objectives must be identified. The writing of objectives is a highly specific procedure popularized by Mager (1962). Objectives specify outcomes for a training program and help the instructional developer know exactly what skills or knowledge are to be learned. This step is essential to avoid ambiguous content or extraneous content in a training program.

Fifth, an analysis of the actual learners or participants must be performed. This analysis helps the trainer to determine the size of learning groups and determine how participants will be selected and sequenced through the training program or system.

Sixth, the trainer designs a program that makes the best use of time, topics, instructional methods, aids, media, materials, equipment, and instructors. The design of programs in training in business and industry has been influenced markedly by the concept of andragogy, the art and science of adult learning (Knowles, 1970). The assumptions of andragogy specify that education for adults should (1) recognize the experience of adults; (2) be problem-oriented; (3) have immediate application; (4) recognize that adults' self-concept is one of increasing self-directedness and independence; and (5) recognize that adults' readiness for learning is a product of their social life-roles rather than their biological development.

The seventh step in the training process is planning for evaluation and measurement. Evaluation involves establishing baseline data by utilizing appropriate measurement techniques and then determining at the conclusion of a program what participants have learned. Measurement also refers to the evaluation of the program itself and the assessment of the likelihood that the same results will be obtained each time the program is conducted.

Step eight in the training process is the administration of the learning program. Contingency planning is very important, and trainers must attempt to determine all the possible pitfalls to success—before, during, and after the program. Many things can go wrong, and the way the program is administered can determine how well learning occurs.

The ninth step in the training process is the reporting of the results to the business organization. Many federal rules and regulations regarding affirmative action and equal opportunity require that businesses report their results to the federal government.

The tenth and final step is the assessment of organizational achievement. At this time, the trainer must determine whether the funds of the organization were well invested in training. The basis for this determination lies in the organizational performance analysis and training integration planning made during steps one and two.

If these ten steps are properly employed and documented, then judgments can readily be made regarding the contribution the training effort has made to solving a particular organizational performance problem or achieving a business goal. Whenever training is undertaken, these ten steps occur, although sometimes they happen very quickly and sometimes a step requires months of effort. Whatever the case, decisions must be made at each of the ten steps.

Human Resources Development

During the last ten years, the profession of training has become known in some circles as human resources development (Nadler, 1970). The trainer is viewed as having at least three roles: learning specialist, consultant, and administrator. The concept of human resources development has become so pervasive that *Training Magazine,* the largest publication in the field, has adopted the subtitle *The Magazine of Human Resource Development.* Similarly, the American Society for Training and Development (ASTD), the largest professional association of trainers, gives special recognition to human resources development in the foreword to its handbook (Craig, 1976).

Training in business and industry has now emerged as the profession of human resources development. It is characterized by professional societies, special publications, a growing list of books describing the application of behavioral science theory, instructional technology, and the science of program and materials development. It seems that no one discipline is responsible for the growth of the profession. Rather, training has drawn what it needs from education, law, psychology, philosophy, sociology, the physical sciences, and mathematics.

It is likely that human resources development will continue to expand dramatically for several reasons. First, trainers are now developing better theory and skills; second, organizations are becoming more complex and stressful, requiring individuals to continue their development to cope with the social and technical changes required for job success; and third, a large number of executives have had positive experiences with human resources development, and they understand that training can be an effective part of a corporate strategy to solve organizational problems and increase productivity and efficiency.

Chapter Nine

The Future of Human Resources Development

Donald F. Seaman
Donnie Dutton

One cannot accurately determine the extent of training opportunities in the United States, for almost everyone appears to be involved in training in some form. There are no accurate records of the total number of participants in training programs or the amount of money expended in those efforts. Estimates based partially on available records are usually the best approximations that can be produced.

Before we explore the opportunities that exist in training, let us differentiate several terms that are often used in regard to instructional activity in business and industry. The following definitions are drawn from Drawbough (1975, p. 14). *Education* usually refers to learning experiences such as classroom instruction, field trips, and other cognitive activities. *Personal and human resources development* seem to imply the improvement of the whole person, including the affective domain. *Organizational development* is a process that is sustained over a long time for the purpose of improving the effectiveness of an organization. *Training,* the most popular term, usually refers to an on-the-job experience for skilled workers that lasts a short time and is relatively inexpensive.

Although these definitions may appear adequate, Drawbough notes that the term *training* is slowly yielding to such terms as *personal development* and *human resources development,* terms which more adequately denote instruction in the cognitive and affective domains as well as in psychomotor skills. This change is further emphasized by Sutton (1977), who indicates that training is but one function in a system for the development of human resources. He recommends that the training function involve the development of individual talents so that people can not only perform their work assignment but also achieve their own career goals as well as meet the future needs of the organization that employs them.

Scope of Human Resources Development

Because of the changing philosophy and attitudes toward the concept of training, the number of individuals involved in some sort of training or human resources development program has increased rapidly during the past few years. Although Ginsburg and Hepburn (1972) indicate that the total training structure in the United States is so diffuse that no one can see its entirety, there are some data regarding the size and scope of this mushrooming enterprise in various sectors of the labor force.

Business and Industry. There is no doubt that business and industry contribute more, in both financial resources and number of participants, to human resources development programs than any other sponsors in the United States. However, no precise data are available. The lowest estimate indicates that 7,500 companies spend a total of $2 billion a year for formal, business-sponsored learning experiences for some four million employees (Killingsworth, 1977, p. 2). It appears that the biggest spenders for these learning activities are financial institutions, utilities, and transportation and communication firms.

Drawbough (1975) determined that the total pool of potential trainees in the major industries (private, nonagricultural, nongovernment establishments) numbered 57,836,000 in 1974, and he estimates that the total expenditure for training activities for that year was between $20 and $25 billion. If those figures seem somewhat staggering, Tracey (1974, p. 46) states that "It is estimated that in excess of $32 billion was invested in training in 1971. The sum represents 3.1 percent of the gross national product in that year, and it does not include the funds spent for public and private education or disbursed by the federal government for support to elementary, secondary, and higher education."

Research by Lundberg, Dunbar, and Bayless (1973) also documents the extent of training in business and industry. From a survey related to contemporary management training, the investigators found that 93 percent of all responding firms had training programs. In addition, companies without their own personnel development programs met their needs through university programs and management education courses offered by consulting organizations, and by attracting managers and executives from other corporations. However, in viewing the scope of training from another perspective, the same research study found approximately 18,000 trade associations and consultants and more than 2,000 private and public educational institutions that conduct various types of training seminars throughout the United States.

In a discussion about the scope of training, or human resources development, one must consider not only the amount but also the kind of training available. As most readers would probably expect, much of the learning focuses upon improving personnel so they can function better in their work roles, especially in administrative and managerial positions. But employees have their purposes also. According to one author, "Corporations train employees for corporation benefits; employees enroll . . . to improve their own positions" (Drawbough, 1975, p. 11). In articles, books, and related publications on training, such terms as *assertiveness training, performance feedback,* and *total human resources development system* appear repeatedly. In addition, opportunities for training are not limited to employees.

Educational programs sponsored by business and industry are also extended occasionally to serve groups of people outside of the organizational structure, such as the families of employees, students, retired persons, the disadvantaged, the handicapped, and the general public (Drawbough, 1975).

Why is there so much concern for human resources development, particularly when the scope of the enterprise is virtually impossible to assess? According to Byers (1970, p. 11), "The 1967 Presidential Task Force on Career Advancement was impressed to find that all ten of the companies found by a jury of 300 highly placed industry executives to be the best managed in the United States had active, continuing management development programs. . . . The Task Force members believed this is no coincidence."

Federal Government. Taking notice of the success of business and industry in human resources development, the federal government has not been lax in instituting its own training programs. According to Ginsburg and Hepburn (1972, p. 32), the Government Employee Training Act of 1958 gave the Civil Service Commission basic responsibility for promoting and co-ordinating training and development programs for federal employees. By 1971, a total of 108 training centers had been established in thirty states, Washington, D.C., the Canal Zone, and some foreign countries.

Because the number of federal agencies, bureaus, and related entities is quite large, exact figures on the scope of training programs are difficult, if not impossible, to obtain. Even the claim of national security prohibits the release of certain data. However, Ginsburg and Hepburn (1972) report that 7,035 government personnel were assigned to full-time training and training-support duties (mostly development officers and instructors) in 1971. They also indicate that almost two thirds of all federal workers were participating in training, at an estimated cost of $838 million that year. Among the topics of training were executive development, labor relations, instructor training, correction and law enforcement, secretarial and office skills, and medical and health training.

Military. Probably no other organization depends upon

the success of its training programs as much as does the military (Carr and Ripley, 1980). From the day a recruit is inducted into a branch of the military service, he receives training of all kinds: basic training, unit training, and specific skills training. An inductee may spend up to six months in training before being permanently assigned to a unit. The military also provides training and education for noncommissioned officers and regular officers through command and staff colleges, Reserve Officer Training Corps on college campuses, and the military academies.

As weapon systems become more complicated, high-quality training becomes even more crucial for the military. Thus, the development of materials and programs for training receives high priority in the military, which sometimes calls on outside agencies for assistance in that activity. Spangenburg (1971) offers evidence that military training manuals are usually designed to assist military personnel in selecting and implementing a specific approach to achieving specific training goals, whether they be the recall of facts, acquisition of motor and reactive skills, acquisition of concepts, problem solving, decision making, or putting attitudes into practice. The military's complex and often expensive training programs are estimated to cost in excess of $3 billion dollars annually (Drawbough, 1975).

Government-Sponsored Work and Training Programs. Since the early 1960s, a variety of federal, state, regional, and local governments have sponsored and implemented work and training programs. Some of these were terminated due to lack of success, withdrawal of funding, or political pressures. Among the more notable of these programs, enacted by federal legislation, are the Neighborhood Youth Corps (NYC), Work Incentive Program (WIN), Job Corps, and those programs funded by the Manpower Development Training Act (MDTA) and the Comprehensive Employment and Training Act (CETA).

Although accurate estimates of funds expended for all these programs are difficult to attain, Tracey (1974) calculates that funds provided for NYC, WIN, and the Job Corps programs in 1971 totaled $1.4 billion. One can only assume that current expenditures are substantially higher not only because of inflation but also because the unemployment rate is now higher than in 1971 and new Job Corps Centers have been approved. If one includes government-sponsored training programs such as those conducted by the Cooperative Extension Service and local governments, as well as those sponsored by state governments, one cannot begin to make an estimate of the cost: the vastness of the operation is beyond dispute.

The Challenges of the Future

Attempts to forecast trends in training usually take a relatively conservative approach and address the subject of opportunities for training in the next ten to fifteen years. As Toffler (1974) indicates, most educational futurists do not agree on terminology, much less on their predictions. Consequently, our discussion of anticipated trends may raise as many questions as it answers. Forecasts are necessarily based on interpretations of current information, and any group of forecasters is apt to interpret differently the same data. Our projections are based on data regarding demographic trends; political, social, and economic changes; and technological products and innovations. We anticipate eight trends in training and present and discuss each briefly.

Business and industry will intensify human resources development programs during the next several years. Although these programs are becoming more expensive and time-consuming to formulate and implement, the returns for the investment seem to warrant an increase: "There appears to be no diminishment of industry's enthusiasm for training programs. Rather, all signs indicate that the future will see more of them than did the past" (Barton-Dobenin and Hodgetts, 1975, p. 35).

Substantial federal government support will be provided for training programs. As social service programs increase in volume and in stature, additional personnel will be needed to train the staff necessary for their implementation. In essence, bureaucracies are people, and they can grow only through the acquisition of personnel. In addition, personnel must be trained in order to implement new and changing programs of government agencies. For example, the concept of regionalism in government decision making for local communities is becoming wide-ly accepted in the United States ("What Life Will Be Like . . . ," 1977). However, in order for the concept to be successful, gov-ernment decision makers must be trained to think in terms of regional issues, problems that transcend local situations and cross state lines. Therefore, training people to accept new ideas and ways of thinking is even more crucial to government than ever before and will increase in importance in years to come.

Apprenticeship programs will increase substantially, par-ticularly in agencies outside of business and industry. Already, within the realm of business and industry, apprenticeship train-ing is on the increase. More than 100,000 Americans entered formal apprenticeship programs in nearly 400 trades in 1976, and the number was larger in 1977 (Porter, 1977). However, as the territories served by an increasing number of agencies and organizations become more diffused, apprenticeships (or intern-ships) of employees between and among agencies will increase. Annual reports, joint planning conferences, and occasional cooperative efforts will no longer suffice. Actual on-the-job ex-periences of even highly trained personnel will become more common. According to Lippitt (1975, p. 49), "There will be a need for a more effective interface among government, educa-tion, and industry. Interchanging personnel among these organi-zational systems will increase as problems intensify."

The search for energy technologies will cause shifts as well as increases in demands for training programs. Currently, government and industry are examining solar energy and new methods for coal production. Solar heating systems are being commercially produced, and various federal agencies are fund-ing experimental projects. The need for trained personnel for development, testing, and installation is substantial. At the same time, the coal industry is beginning to achieve phenomenal growth after years of decline. The coal industry is expected to experience significant growth, "requiring trained . . . supervisors of which there is an industry shortage. Between now and 1985, it is estimated that the industry will need a total of 3,705 more technicians, 1,140 more engineers and 1,995 surveyors. Within the same period an estimated total of 5,400 salaried employees will be needed" (Killingsworth, 1977, p. 1). As other new or re-vitalized industries grow and develop in response to energy needs, their needs for training will be commensurate with their development.

Greater efforts will be expended toward staff develop-ment and training in colleges and universities. A study con-ducted by the Educational Testing Service ("Colleges Respond . . . ," 1977) indicates a lack of participation in developmental activities by faculty at colleges and universities throughout the United States. The interest generated by this study led offi-cials in some states to examine this topic and to attempt to eval-uate programs now being offered. As college costs continue to increase, pressures from students, parents, legislators, and the public will cause higher education administrators to become in-creasingly concerned with the quality of teaching at their insti-tutions. Whether training and development programs will im-prove that quality remains to be seen; however, as long as peo-ple believe it will, and most seem to believe it, this area of training will show a marked increase in years to come.

Professional associations will require greater amounts of training for purposes of certification, or accreditation, or both. This trend, which began several years ago, received added im-petus from the development and acceptance of the *continuing education unit* (CEU). The medical profession, in particular, has felt the pressure to keep abreast of new practices, and there are increasing signs that others in the health field may be compelled to follow with compulsory continuing education. "The debate over the merits of voluntary versus mandatory continuing edu-cation is becoming louder as professional boards and legislatures demand completion of current courses as evidence of profes-sional competence" ("Nurses Meet . . . ," 1977, p. 8). If the medical profession is moving toward emphasizing continuing education, other professions will soon follow. This aspect of hu-man resources development will become extremely important in the near future.

Advances in educational curricula will require a continu-ously retrained cadre at all levels of educational institutions. Re-cent advances in the curricula offered by some public high schools make it conceivable that a system allowing for a complete year of retraining on a regular basis for all school personnel will be commonplace in the future. For example, simulated lunar landings in a setting that looks like a space control center are part of a physics class at Northern Community High School in Flint, Michigan. "Kids used to have to wait until graduate school to get this," according to one teacher ("What Life Will Be . . . ," 1977, p. 79). With the increasing use of computers and other devices in colleges and schools, the demand for better-trained users as well as developers is imminent. College and university degrees will surely acquire a more temporary status as indicators of educational accomplishment in contrast with the more permanent status traditionally accorded them.

Societal changes will demand formal as well as informal training in areas that are relatively new or that have not been developed previously. Some of these social needs are likely to include training for citizen board members as more decisions are made by citizen advisory groups; programs to promote better relationships among various ethnic and minority groups; and training for professionals involved in new physical and biomedical technologies (test-tube conception, mandatory metrics, hospices, and thanatology). We expect the current concern for environmental and occupational safety to continue, and this concern will require new specialized training; for example, a new field of industrial hygiene to protect workers' health in the workplace. As the mean age of people in this country continues to rise, the demand for trained specialists for aging centers will increase. Longer life spans, earlier retirements, and more positive social attitudes toward aging will demand professionals who are creative, active, and dedicated to working with older people. Finally, training will be required in fields yet undreamed of.

In essence, training in the future will be influenced by many changes—political, educational, social, and technological—which are occurring and which will continue. Training needs and opportunities may neither resemble nor appear to be related to present ones, but individuals who seek to acquire new knowledge or skills will find many opportunities.

Solutions to problems come in many forms. Problem

solving also benefits from suggestions that help one go beyond self-imposed mental boundaries. Therefore, in conclusion, we offer a caution: "Ancient weathermen studied entrails and some of today's meteorologists believe that no method of long-range forecasting developed since is much better" ("Weather Forecasts . . . ," 1978, p. 46). Although this conclusion may be difficult to accept in an era of weather satellites and sophisticated apparatus, it highlights the uncertainties inherent in any forecasting. But regardless of whether our predictions prove to be accurate, the practice of forecasting—involving analytic and interpretive consideration of our present situation and goals—seems worthwhile.

Postscript

Stanley M. Grabowski

Whatever else one says about training, it is undeniably a big business that involves enormous outlays of money and engages almost every conceivable kind of institution, organization, or agency. Different labels are used to describe the same generic programs, models, and approaches with slight variations in their application to specific needs and circumstances. This diversity of need and sponsorship makes it difficult to attain a descriptive or evaluative overview of the field of training.

The purpose and need for training determine the nature of any specific training program, but other factors also influence the training process. The nature of the organization and the nature of the trainees have a profound effect on the level, duration, extent, and kind of training undertaken. For example, preservice training for professionals usually includes formal preparation in a degree program with some additional internship experience, whereas in-service training for nonprofessionals may be informal and brief. Thus some kinds of training are formal, such as that offered by colleges, universities, and professional schools; others are informal, such as workshops and self-directed learning, and are not part of a degree program nor for credit.

Similarly, some training is performed entirely in-house, by employing organizations or agencies; other training is offered by organizations whose sole mission is to provide education and training. Indeed, many people and institutions have entered the lucrative field of training. Institutions of higher education have long been involved in preservice education and recently have entered the continuing education field as well. Proprietary schools have been preparing individuals for various occupations for a long time. But, increasingly, individual consultants and consulting firms have moved into the training market.

In the case of volunteers, they generally receive no preservice training, but some training is provided on the job. Between the rigorous and extended training for professionals and the relatively scant training for volunteers, there are other configurations such as a core preservice training program followed by in-service education for paraprofessionals and various formats for continuing education in many jobs and in virtually all the professions.

Until recent years, each organization or agency found its own way in training. Now the fundamental similarities among various types of training are recognized, and many trainers see a value in working closely with others to advance the state of the art of training. The prevalence of the term *human resources development* is one indication that commonalties exist which can be addressed in concert. As a result, there is an increasing acknowledgment that the training of trainers is properly the province of adult educators who have special competencies in this area.

Training is conducted by various individuals with differing primary responsibilities. Some are specifically designated as teachers, trainers, instructors, staff developers, or human resources developers. Others perform the training function although they may not call it that; administrators, supervisors, and managers fall into this category. In a sense, journal editors and book publishers are trainers inasmuch as they provide information that can improve the skills and knowledge of their readership. Salespeople, in explaining their products or services, are also engaged in a type of training. The kind and amount of formal and informal training these various individuals have as trainers vary dramatically and have an effect on the training they perform.

The purposes of training include the preparation of individuals to perform tasks, to improve their performance and effectiveness, to keep up with developments lest their skills become obsolescent, and to satisfy requirements. In addition, training can serve the purpose of socializing individuals so that they can best respond to an organization's needs.

Everyone is interested, in one way or another, in better and more effective use of human resources. Organizations, institutions, and agencies are affected by the amount and kind of training their managers, employees, and volunteers receive. Specifically, training influences stability and change within organizations.

The quality and type of training in the professions has an even more serious effect on society. The service professions, including medicine, nursing, teaching, law, social work, and the ministry, not only affect individual clients but also have an influence on the fabric of our society. In these areas of professionalization, consumers have voiced their concern, which has led to the legislation of mandatory continuing education for many service professionals. Whether or not continuing education for professionals will continue to be mandated by legislation, professionals' need for continuing learning will persist. Professionals, recognizing their need, may well choose to satisfy more of their need for continuing education through self-directed learning.

All the authors who contributed to this book provide evidence that training is entering a new phase. Although there are still some contradictions, confusion, and criticisms of what presently passes for training, practitioners in the field are working toward more systematic analyses and are coordinating their efforts across disciplines and institutional settings. One of the healthiest signs of change is that faculties in professional schools are now reconsidering the way they have traditionally taught and prepared individuals for their respective fields. They are, at least, admitting that the traditional preparation may not be the only, or necessarily the best, way to train professionals. The principles and practices of adult education are slowly beginning to gain acceptance in many academic and preprofessional fields.

Some trainers who espouse principles of adult education have been constrained from implementing them to the degree they would like. Often the press of time and the pressure to train large numbers of people without adequate resources have forced trainers to adopt pragmatic rather than theoretical or idealistic approaches. But as is evident from reading this book and other current literature on training, the situation is changing. Trainers are being given assistance in developing theoretical support to move them beyond their purely pragmatic approaches.

The interdisciplinary exchange of literature, first given an impetus by the Educational Resources Information Center (ERIC) Clearinghouse on Adult Education at Syracuse University between 1967 and 1973, has been continued by journal editors and a few publishers. Some national conferences of various associations sponsor joint meetings or invite members from each other's associations to participate. Comparative continuing education is an area receiving increasing attention from scholars and trainers alike. Economic as well as ideological exigencies are forcing continuing educators to devise new patterns of helping professionals meet their educational needs.

As technological changes escalate, creating jobs not previously envisioned, the needs for more trainers and more training are bound to increase. Furthermore, the already large and steadily increasing numbers of individuals who make career changes several times during their work lives all require learning and training. These trends create a great demand for more and diverse kinds of training, and these trends are expected to continue at least into the next century.

This book was designed to offer a picture of the present status of training with some predictions for the future. The authors raise numerous questions that demand the attention of leaders in training and other aspects of adult education. Some of these questions are of concern to all who are involved in, responsible for, or concerned about training. Among these questions are: What is the purpose of training? What are the functions of the training system? What is the solution to motivating professionals to continue their education? Other questions are specific to discrete organizations or to individuals serving in a particular training role: How can one best train part-time teachers of adults working in adult basic education? Which techniques are most cost-effective in training within business and industry?

Training, despite its shortcomings as a field of study, holds out a challenge and an adventure to those who understand its value and importance. Together with the problems and headaches, training brings a certain degree of satisfaction unmatched by many other kinds of work. Both current practitioners and individuals now entering this field can rest assured that they will not exhaust the many opportunities of developing and refining their chosen field of work.

References

Adelson, M. *Professional Competence Core.* Arlington, Va.: Documentary Reproduction Service, 1972. ED 072764, HE 003865

Aker, G. F. "Criteria for Evaluating Graduate Study in Adult Education." Unpublished manuscript, University of Chicago, Center for Continuing Education, no date.

Anderson, G. L. *Trends in Education for the Professions.* AAHE/ERIC/Higher Education Research Report No. 7. Washington, D.C.: American Association for Higher Education, 1974.

Apps, H. W. "Tomorrow's Adult Educator—Some Thoughts and Questions." *Adult Education,* 1972, *22* (3), 218-226.

Argyris, C., and Schön, D. A. *Theory in Practice: Increasing Professional Effectiveness.* San Francisco: Jossey-Bass, 1974.

Asimow, M. *Introduction to Design.* Englewood Cliffs, N.J.: Prentice-Hall, 1962.

Barnes, L. B. "Approaches to Organizational Change." In W. G. Bennis, K. D. Benne, and R. Chin (Eds.), *The Planning of Change.* (2nd ed.) New York: Holt, Rinehart and Winston, 1969.

Barton-Dobenin, J., and Hodgetts, R. M. "Management Training Programs: Who Uses Them and Why?" *Training and Development Journal,* 1975, *29* (3), 34-35, 37-40.

Becker, S. *The Training Process.* Boston: Learncom, Inc., 1978.

Beder, H. "An Environmental Interaction Model for Agency Development in Adult Education." *Adult Education,* 1978, *28* (3), 176-190.

Bender, L. W., and Bender, R. L. "Part-Time Teachers: 'Step Children' of the Community College." *Community College Review,* 1973, *1,* 29-37.

Benne, K. D., Chin, R., and Bennis, W. G. "Science and Practice." In W. G. Bennis, K. D. Benne, and R. Chin (Eds.), *The Planning of Change.* (2nd ed.) New York: Holt, Rinehart and Winston, 1969.

Blalock, H. M., Jr., and Blalock, A. B. *Methodology in Social Research.* New York: McGraw-Hill, 1968.

Blumer, H. "The Problem of the Concept in Social Psychology." *American Journal of Sociology,* 1940, *45* (5), 707-719.

Bossel, H. "College Student and Dropout Problem: A Quantitative Dynamic Simulation." *Instructional Science,* 1974, *3* (1), 23-50.

Boston University School of Education. *Women's Leadership Project in Adult Education: Final Report.* Bethesda, Md.: ERIC Document Reproduction Service, 1975.   ED 117 447

Boulding, K. E. *The Image.* Ann Arbor: University of Michigan Press, 1956.

Boyd, R. D. "New Designs for Adult Education Doctoral Programs." *Adult Education,* 1969, *19* (3), 186-196.

Boyette, R., Blount, W., and Petaway, K. "The Plight of the New Careerist." *American Journal of Orthopsychiatry,* 1971, *41,* 237-238.

Broadbeck, M. "Logic and Scientific Method in Research on Teaching." In N. L. Gage (Ed.), *Handbook of Research on Teaching.* Chicago: Rand McNally, 1963.

Bromley, D. B. *The Psychology of Human Ageing.* Baltimore: Penguin Books, 1966.

Brooks, H. "Dilemmas in Engineering Education." *IEEE Spectrum,* 1967, *4* (2), 89-91.

Brown, W. F. "Effectiveness of Paraprofessionals: The Evidence." *Personnel and Guidance Journal,* 1974, *53* (4), 257-263.

Bruny, S. P. "Educational and Experimental Backgrounds of

Adult Educators in Franklin County, Ohio, and Their Training Needs." Unpublished doctoral dissertation, Ohio State University, 1970.

Bunge, M. "Technology as Applied Science." *Technology and Culture,* 1966, *7* (3), 329-347.

Bunge, M. "The Role of Forecast in Planning." *Theory and Decision,* 1973, *3* (3), 207-221.

Bunning, R. L. *Skills and Knowledges for the Adult Educator: A Delphi Study.* Washington, D.C.: Adult Education Association of the U.S.A., 1976. ED 123394

Byers, K. T. *Employee Training and Development in the Public Service.* Chicago: Public Personnel Association, 1970.

Cameron, C., Rockhill, K., and Wright, J. "Certification: An Examination of the Issue by and for Adult Educators." Position paper prepared for the Commission of Professors of Adult Education by the Task Force on Certification, 1976.

Carr, T. W., and Ripley, R. M. "Armed Forces and Veterans' Education." In E. J. Boone, R. W. Shearon, E. E. White, and Associates (Eds.), *Serving Personal and Community Needs Through Adult Education.* San Francisco: Jossey-Bass, 1980.

Carter, G. L. "Development of a Conceptual Formulation for Determining Curricula for the Practitioner: A Case." Paper presented to Adult Education Research Conference, Chicago, April 1974.

Carter, L. F. "Knowledge Production and Utilization in Contemporary Organizations." In T. L. Eidell and L. M. Kitchel (Eds.), *Knowledge Production and Utilization in Educational Administration.* Eugene: University of Oregon Press, 1968.

Cassidy, H. G. "The Problem of the Sciences and the Humanities." *American Scientist,* 1960, *48* (3), 383-398.

Chamberlain, M. "The Professional Adult Educator." Unpublished doctoral dissertation, Education Department, University of Chicago, 1960.

Chamberlain, M. "The Competencies of Adult Educators." *Adult Education,* 1961, *11,* 78-82.

Charters, A. N. "Continuing Education for the Professions." In R. M. Smith, G. F. Aker, and J. R. Kidd (Eds.), *Handbook of Adult Education.* New York: Macmillan, 1970.

Checkland, P. B. "The Development of Systems Thinking by

Systems Practice—A Methodology from an Action-Research Program." In R. Trappl (Ed.), *Progress in Cybernetics and Systems Research.* Vol. 2. Washington, D.C.: Hemisphere Publishing, 1975.

Churchman, C. W. *The Systems Approach.* New York: Dell, 1968.

"Colleges Respond to Public Demands for Improved Instruction." *ETS Developments,* 1977, *24,* 4-5.

Commission of Professors of Adult Education. *Adult Education: Outlines of an Emerging Field of University Study.* (G. Jensen, A. A. Liveright, and W. Hallenbeck, Eds.) Washington, D.C.: Adult Education Association of the U.S.A., 1964.

Confer, S. H. "A Study of Volunteer Value Systems." Unpublished manuscript, Washington, D.C., 1971.

Confer, S. H. "Evaluation of CWA's Newly Elected Officers' Training." Unpublished manuscript, Washington, D.C., 1973.

Confer, S. H. "Local Leadership Week-Long Conference Evaluation." Unpublished manuscript, Washington, D.C., 1975.

Confer, S. H. "Characteristics of Volunteer Trainers." Unpublished manuscript, Washington, D.C., 1980.

Conrath, C. "Government, an Active Partner." In L. W. Natress, Jr. (Ed.), *Continuing Education for the Professions.* Chicago: Natresources, Inc., 1970.

Consortium of Florida Adult Educators and Practitioners. *Competencies for Adult Educators and an Assessment Inventory.* Tallahassee: Adult Education Department, University of Florida, 1976.

Cooper, J. A. D. " 'Continuing Education'—What Do We Mean by It and Why Is It Important?" *Journal of Medical Education,* 1974, *49,* 617-619.

Craig, R. L. (Ed.). *Training and Development Handbook, a Guide to Human Resource Development.* (2nd ed.) New York: McGraw-Hill, 1976.

Curriculum Research and Development Center of the University of Rhode Island. *Region I ABE Staff Development Evaluation.* Kingston: University of Rhode Island, 1975.

Dave, R. H. "The Identification and Measurement of Environmental Variables that Are Related to Educational Achievement." Unpublished doctoral dissertation, Education Department, University of Chicago, 1963.

Davison, C. "Training Needs of Instructors in Adult Basic Education Programs in British Columbia." Unpublished manuscript, Adult Education Research Centre, University of British Columbia, Vancouver, 1970.

DeLancy, P. *The Licensing of Professions in West Virginia.* Chicago: Foundation Press, 1938.

Delworth, U., and Brown, W. F. "The Paraprofessional as a Member of the College Guidance Team." In A. Gartner, V. C. Jackson, and F. Riessman (Eds.), *Paraprofessionals in Education Today.* New York: Human Sciences Press, 1977.

DeSanctis, V. "Staff Development in Adult Education: An Evolving Process." In G. Spear (Ed.), *Adult Education Staff Development: Selected Issues, Alternatives and Implications.* Kansas City, Mo.: Center for Resource Development in Adult Education, 1976.

Dewey, J. *The Sources of a Science of Education.* New York: Liveright, 1929.

Dewey, J. *Democracy and Education.* New York: Macmillan, 1937.

Dewey, J. *The Quest for Certainty.* New York: Putnam's, 1960. (Originally published 1929.)

Dickerman, W. "Implications of This Book for Programs of Graduate Study in Adult Education." In G. Jensen, A. A. Liveright, and W. Hallenbeck (Eds.), *Adult Education: Outlines of an Emerging Field of University Study.* Washington, D.C.: Adult Education Association of the U.S.A., 1964.

Dill, W. R. "Obsolescence as a Problem of Personal Initiative." In S. Dubin (Ed.), *Professional Obsolescence.* Lexington, Mass.: Heath, 1972.

D'Onofrio, C. N. "Aides—Pain or Panacea?" *Public Health Reports,* 1970, *85* (9), 788-801.

Douglah, M. A., and Moss, G. "Adult Education as a Field of Study and Its Implications for the Preparation of Adult Educators." *Adult Education,* 1969, *19* (2), 127-134.

Drawbough, C. C. *An Overview of Personnel Development in Business and Industry.* Columbus: Ohio State University, Center for Vocational Education, 1975.

Eldredge, R. G. "Associations, in the Thick of the Problem." In L. W. Natress, Jr. (Ed.), *Continuing Education for the Professions.* Chicago: Natresources, Inc., 1970.

Eley, L. W. "Universities, the Seat of the Experts." In L. W. Natress, Jr. (Ed.), *Continuing Education for the Professions.* Chicago: Natresources Inc., 1970.

Engelbrecht, W. M. "Follow-Up on Paraprofessionals Working with Low-Income Families." Unpublished doctoral dissertation, Department of Community Service Education, Cornell University, 1972.

Essert, P. L. "A Proposed New Program in Adult Education." *Adult Education,* 1960, *10* (3), 131-140.

Feaster, J. G. *Impact of the Expanded Food and Nutrition Education Program on Low-Income Families: An Indepth Analysis.* Agriculture Economic Report No. 220. Washington, D.C.: U.S. Government Printing Office, 1972.

Fenn, N. E., Jr. "The Identification of Competencies Pertinent to the Certification of Teachers in Adult Basic Education." Unpublished doctoral dissertation, Florida State University, 1972.

Finan, J. L. "The Systems Concept as a Principle of Methodological Decision." In R. M. Gagne (Ed.), *Psychological Principles in Systems Development.* New York: Holt, Rinehart and Winston, 1962.

Flexner, A. "Is Social Work a Profession?" *School and Society,* 1915, *1,* 901-911.

Florida State University, Department of Adult Education. "Southeastern Institute for Teacher Training in ABE." Tallahassee: Department of Adult Education, Florida State University, 1968. ED 061 480

Fores, M. "Price, Technology, and the Paper Model." *Technology and Culture,* 1971, *12* (4), 621-627.

Fraenkel, J. R. *Helping Students Think and Value: Strategies for Teaching the Social Studies.* Englewood Cliffs, N.J.: Prentice-Hall, 1973.

Freed, A. M. Z. "Design and Operation of a Plan of Action for Developing One Component (Valence) of a System for Controlling Withdrawal from an Adult Basic Education Program in a Community College." Unpublished doctoral dissertation, Program of Postsecondary Education, Florida State University, 1977.

Freidson, E. "Dominant Professions, Bureaucracy, and Client Services." In R. Rosengreen and M. Lefton (Eds.), *Organizations and Clients: Essays in the Sociology of Service.* Columbus, Ohio: Merrill, 1970.

Friedmann, J. *Retracking America.* Garden City, N.Y.: Anchor Press/Doubleday, 1973.

Frye, R. E. "The Expanded Food and Nutrition Education Program." Paper presented at 1971 National Agricultural Outlook Conference, Washington, D.C., Feb. 1971.

Gartner, A., and Riessman, F. "The Paraprofessional Movement in Perspective." *Personnel and Guidance Journal,* 1974, *53* (4), 253-256.

Ginsburg, E., and Hepburn, A. B. "The Role of Training in National Manpower Policy." *Training and Development Journal,* 1972, *26* (7), 30-34.

Grabowski, S. *Training Teachers of Adults: Models and Innovative Programs.* Syracuse, N.Y.: National Association for Public Continuing and Adult Education and ERIC Clearinghouse in Career Education, 1976.

Grattan, C. H. *In Quest of Knowledge: A Historical Perspective on Adult Education.* New York: Arno Press, 1971.

Graves, C. W. "Deterioration of Work Standards." *Harvard Business Review,* 1966, *44* (5), 117-126.

Griffith, W. S., and Cloutier, G. H. *A Directory and Analysis of Degree Programs for Preparing Professional Adult Educators in the United States.* Chicago: Department of Education, University of Chicago, 1972. ED 058540

Gross, B. *The Managing of Organizations.* Vol. 2. New York: Free Press, 1964.

Gross, R., and Osterman, P. (Eds.). *The New Professionals.* New York: Simon & Schuster, 1972.

Grosser, C., Henry, W. E., and Kelly, J. G. (Eds.). *Nonprofessionals in the Human Services.* San Francisco: Jossey-Bass, 1969.

Hardcastle, D. "The Indigenous Nonprofessional in the Social

Service Bureaucracy: A Critical Examination." *Social Work,* 1971, *16* (2), 56-57.

Harless, J. *Behavior Analysis and Management.* Champaign, Ill.: Stipes, 1970.

Harris, D. A., and Parsons, M. H. *Adjunct Faculty, A Working System of Development.* Hagerstown, Md.: Hagerstown Junior College, 1975. ED 115 318

Hartstead, P., and Venner, H. "Project to Utilize Volunteers in Eliminating Adult Illiteracy, Quarterly Progress Report, First Quarter." Bethesda, Md.: ERIC Document Reproduction Service, 1970. ED 047 238

Havelock, R. G. *The Change Agent's Guide to Innovation in Education.* Englewood Cliffs, N.J.: Educational Technology Publications, 1973.

Hawaii University. "Experimental Training Program in ABE in Correctional Institutions." Honolulu: Hawaii University, 1970. ED 068 788

Hertzberg, F. *Work and the Nature of Man.* New York: Crowell, 1966.

Hoffman, H., and Pagano, J. "A New Conceptual Model for Adult Basic Education Staff Training with Applications to Corrections, New Careers, and Migrant Education." In G. Spear (Ed.), *Adult Education Staff Development: Selected Issues, Alternatives, and Implications.* Kansas City, Mo.: Center for Resource Development in Adult Education, 1976.

Houle, C. O. "Professional Education for Educators of Adults." *Adult Education,* 1956, *6* (3), 134-136.

Houle, C. O. "The Role of Continuing Education in Current Professional Development." *American Library Association Bulletin,* 1967, *61* (3), 259-267.

Houle, C. O. "The Educators of Adults." In R. M. Smith, G. F. Aker, and J. R. Kidd (Eds.), *Handbook of Adult Education.* New York: Macmillan, 1970.

Houle, C. O. *The Design of Education.* San Francisco: Jossey-Bass, 1972.

Houle, C. O. "The Nature of Continuing Professional Education." In R. M. Smith (Ed.), *Adult Learning: Issues and Innovations.* Information Series, No. 8. DeKalb, Ill.: ERIC Clearinghouse in Career Education, 1976.

Houle, C. O. *Continuing Learning in the Professions.* San Francisco: Jossey-Bass, 1980.

Hudson, B., and others. "Knowledge Networks for Educational Planning." Unpublished report, School of Architecture and Urban Planning, University of California, Los Angeles, 1976.

Hughes, E. C. "Education for a Profession." In P. H. Ennis and H. W. Winger (Eds.), *Seven Questions About the Profession of Librarianship.* Chicago: University of Chicago Press, 1962.

Illich, I. *Deschooling Society.* New York: Harrow Books, 1970.

"Important New ASTD Study Will Validate Trainer Competencies." *Adult Education Clearinghouse Newsletter,* 1977, *5* (11), 1.

Ingham, R. J. "Design and Operation of Educative Systems." Unpublished manuscript, Department of Adult Education, Florida State University, 1972.

Ingham, R. J., Munro, B. G., and Massey, R. M. "A Survey of Graduate Programs in Adult Education in the United States and Canada." Unpublished manuscript, Department of Adult Education, Florida State University, 1970.

Ingham, R. J., and Qazilbash, H. "A Survey of Graduate Programs in Adult Education in the United States and Canada." Unpublished manuscript, Department of Adult Education, Florida State University, 1968.

Ingham, R. J., and Robbins, J. N. "Survey of Graduate Programs in the United States and Canada." Unpublished manuscript, Program for the Design and Management of Postsecondary Education, Florida State University, 1977.

James, W. B. "Perceived Utility of Adult Basic Education Teacher Competencies." Unpublished doctoral dissertation, University of Tennessee, 1976.

Jantsch, E. *Design for Evolution.* New York: Braziller, 1975.

Jensen, G. E. "How Adult Education Borrows and Reformulates Knowledge of Other Disciplines." In G. E. Jensen, A. A. Liveright, and W. Hallenbeck (Eds.), *Adult Education: Outlines of an Emerging Field of University Study.* Washington, D.C.: Adult Education Association of the U.S.A., 1964.

Johnstone, W. C., and Rivera, R. J. *Volunteers for Learning.* Chicago: Aldine Press, 1965.

Katz, S. "The Debate over Continuing Medical Education." *Medical Meetings,* Sept. 1979, pp. 6-10.

Killingsworth, C. "Forecast." *CAM Reports: Career Movement and Management Facts,* 1977, *1,* 1-2.

Knowles, M. S. "A General Theory of the Doctorate in Education." *Adult Education,* 1962, *12* (3), 136-141.

Knowles, M. S. *The Modern Practice of Adult Education.* New York: Association Press, 1970.

Knox, A. B. *Development of Adult Education Graduate Programs.* Washington, D.C.: Adult Education Association of the U.S.A., 1973.

Knox, A. B. "Life-Long Self-Directed Education." In A. N. Charters and R. J. Blakely (Eds.), *Fostering the Growing Need to Learn.* Monographs and Annotated Bibliography on Continuing Education and Health Manpower. Rockville, Md.: U.S. Department of Health, Education, and Welfare, Public Health Service, Health Resource Administration, 1974.

Kreitlow, B. *Resources for Staff Development in Adult Basic Education.* Bethesda, Md.: ERIC Document Reproduction Service, 1970. ED 061 482

Kuhling, A. J. "Retention of Volunteers: The Design and Operation of the Cohesion Component of an Explanatory System For Controlling Turnover." Unpublished doctoral dissertation, Florida State University, 1977.

Laird, D. *Approaches to Training and Development.* Reading, Mass.: Addison-Wesley, 1978.

Lang, J., and Burnette, C. "A Model of the Designing Processes." In J. Lang and others (Eds.), *Designing for Human Behavior: Architecture and the Behavioral Sciences.* Stroudsberg, Pa.: Bowden, Hutcheson, and Ross, 1974.

Larrabee, H. A. *Reliable Knowledge.* (Rev. ed.) Boston: Houghton Mifflin, 1964.

Lauffer, A. *The Practice of Continuing Education in the Human Services.* New York: McGraw-Hill, 1977.

Lippitt, G. L. "Training for a Changing World." *Training,* 1975, *12* (5), 46-49.

Liveright, A. A. "The Nature and Aims of Adult Education as a Field of Graduate Study." In G. Jensen, A. A. Liveright, and H. Hallenbeck (Eds.), *Adult Education: Outlines of an*

Emerging Field of University Study. Washington, D.C.: Adult Education Association of the U.S.A., 1964.

Liveright, A. A. *A Study of Adult Education in the United States.* Boston: Center for the Study of Liberal Education for Adults at Boston University, 1968.

Loring, R. "New Trends in Professional Continuing Education." In R. W. Axford (Ed.), *Professional Continuing Education Comes of Age.* Proceedings of a Conference on Professional Continuing Education, Tempe, Ariz., February 1980.

Lundberg, C., Dunbar, R., and Bayless, T. "Contemporary Management Training in Large Corporations." *Training and Development Journal,* 1973, *27* (9), 34-38.

Lynton, R. P., and Pareek, U. *Training for Development.* Homewood, Ill.: Dorsey Press, 1967.

McKendry, N. J. "A Plan of Action to Implement a Program for Retraining Personnel in the Family Practice Residency Program." Unpublished doctoral dissertation, Florida State University, 1979.

Mager, R. F. *Preparing Objectives for Programmed Instruction.* Belmont, Calif.: Fearon, 1962.

Mager, R. F. *Goal Analysis.* Belmont, Calif.: Fearon, 1972.

Mager, R. F., and Pipe, P. *Analyzing Performance Problems.* Belmont, Calif.: Fearon, 1970.

Malmros, A. "Obsolescence of Engineering and Scientific Personnel in Industry." Paper presented at Midwest Conference on Reducing Obsolescence of Engineering Skills, Illinois Institute of Technology, Chicago, 1963.

Malone, V. M. "A Plan of Action to Implement a Job Stability Program for Extension Advisors in an Urban Area." Unpublished doctoral dissertation, Department of Adult Education, Florida State University, 1973.

Marshall, J. C., and Copley, P. O. "Problems of Adult Basic Education Teachers." *Adult Leadership,* 1967, *16* (2), 55-56, 61.

Mayhew, L. B. *Changing Practice in Education for the Professions.* Atlanta: Southern Regional Education Board, 1971.

Mayhew, L. B., and Ford, P. J. *Reform in Graduate and Professional Education.* San Francisco: Jossey-Bass, 1974.

Meehan, E. J. *Explanation in Social Science: A System Paradigm.* Homewood, Ill.: Dorsey Press, 1968.

Mignard, J. E. "Improving Continuing Medical Education." Unpublished paper, Department of Continuing Education,
School of Education, Boston University, 1978.

Miller, G. A., Galanter, D., and Pribram, K. H. *Plans and the
Structure of Behavior.* New York: Holt, Rinehart and Winston, 1960.

Miller, G. E. "Medical Care: Its Social and Organizational Aspects; the Continuing Education of Physicians. *New England
Journal of Medicine,* 1963, *269* (6), 295-299.

Miller, G. E. "Continuing Education for What?" *Journal of
Medical Education,* 1967, *42* (4), 320-326.

Miller, J. "Xerox Builds a New University." *Change Magazine,*
Winter 1973-1974, *15,* 40.

Mitchell, P. H. *Concepts Basic to Nursing.* New York: McGraw-
Hill, 1973.

Mocker, D. W. *A Report on the Identification, Classification,
and Ranking of Competencies Appropriate for Adult Basic
Education Teachers.* Bethesda, Md.: ERIC Document Reproduction Service, 1974. ED 099 469

Morrill, W. H., Oetting, E. R., and Hurst, J. C. "Dimensions of
Counselor Functioning." *Personnel and Guidance Journal,*
1974, *52* (6), 354-359.

Nadler, G. "An Investigation of Design Methodology." *Management Science,* 1967, *13* (10), B-642-655.

Nadler, L. *Developing Human Resources.* Houston: Gulf,
1970.

Nakamoto, J., and Verner, C. *Continuing Education in Medicine: A Review of North American Literature 1960-1970.*
Vancouver: University of British Columbia, 1972.

National Center for Education Statistics. *Participation in
Adult Education, Final Report, 1972.* Washington, D.C.: U.S.
Government Printing Office, 1976.

National Science Foundation. *Knowledge into Action: Improving the Nation's Use of the Social Sciences.* Washington,
D.C.: U.S. Government Printing Office, 1969.

New Human Services Institute. *College Programs for Paraprofessionals: A Directory of Degree-Granting Programs in the Human Services.* New York: Human Sciences Press, 1975.

New York State Education Department. *The Status of Parapro-*

fessionals in New York State School Districts. Albany: New York State Education Department, 1969.

Newell, A., and Simon, H. A. *Human Problem Solving.* Englewood Cliffs, N.J.: Prentice-Hall, 1972.

Newsom, R. W. "Design and Operation of Educative Systems: A Plan of Action to Provide Clear Norms in a System for Controlling Client Participation in an Adult Education Program." Unpublished doctoral dissertation, Program in Postsecondary Education, Florida State University, 1976.

Niemi, J. A., and Davison, C. V. "The Adult Basic Education Teacher: A Model for Analysis of Training." *Continuous Learning,* 1971, *10,* 109-114.

Nixon, A. "Congressional Actions." In C. Grosser, W. E. Henry, and J. G. Kelly (Eds.), *Nonprofessionals in the Human Services.* San Francisco: Jossey-Bass, 1969.

"Nurses Meet Continuing Education Needs with New ETS Program." *ETS Developments,* 1977, *24,* 8.

Nyre, G. F., and Reilly, K. C. *Professional Education in the Eighties: Challenges and Responses.* AAHE/ERIC Higher Education Research Report No. 8. Washington, D.C.: American Association for Higher Education, 1979.

Ostrander, E., Harding, M., and Cheney, M. *Cornell-OEO Project: An Exploration in Urban Extension Activity.* Ithaca: New York State College of Human Ecology, Cornell University, 1971.

"Over 40 Million Hours of Service Given by Seniors." *Aging,* 1978, Nos. 285-286, p. 20.

Pearl, A. "An Analysis and Perspective." In A. Gartner, V. C. Jackson, and F. Riessman (Eds.), *Paraprofessionals in Education Today.* New York: Human Sciences Press, 1977.

Pennington, F. "Program Development in Continuing Professional Education: A Comparative Analysis of Process in Medicine, Social Work, and Teaching." Unpublished doctoral dissertation, Department of Adult Education, University of Illinois, 1975.

Pepper, S. *The Sources of Value.* Berkeley: University of California Press, 1958.

Pirsig, R. M. *Zen and the Art of Motorcycle Maintenance.* New York: Bantam, 1975.

Porter, S. "Apprentices Have Advantages." *Austin American-Statesman,* September 3, 1977.

Porter, L. W., and Speers, R. M. "Organizational, Work, and Personal Factors in Employee Turnover and Absenteeism." *Psychological Bulletin,* 1973, *80* (2), 151-176.

Praxis Corporation. *Performance Analysis Workshop Course Book.* Morristown, N.J.: Praxis, 1970.

Proteus Adult Education Research and Development Team. *Preservice Training Model for TESOL/ABE Teachers and Teacher Aides.* Bethesda, Md.: ERIC Document Reproduction Service, 1969. ED 045 570

Provus, M. *Discrepancy Evaluation: For Educational Program Improvement and Assessment.* Berkeley, Calif.: McCutchan, 1971.

Richards, R. K., Jr. "Current Forces Influencing Continuing Medical Education in the United States." Unpublished doctoral dissertation, University of Michigan, 1975.

Riker, W. H. "Events and Situations." *The Journal of Philosophy,* 1957, *54* (3), 57-70.

Rogers, C. R. *Freedom to Learn: A View of What Education Might Become.* Columbus, Ohio: Merrill, 1968.

Rose, G. "Issues in Professionalism: British Social Work Triumphant." In F. D. Perlmutter (Ed.), *A Design for Social Work Practice.* New York: Columbia University Press, 1974.

Rosenstein, A. B. *A Study of a Profession and Professional Education.* The Final Publication and Recommendations of the UCLA Educational Development Program, Reports Group. Los Angeles: School of Engineering and Applied Science, University of California, 1968. EDP 7-68

Ruesch, J. *Knowledge in Action.* New York: Aronson, 1975.

Schein, E. H., and Kommers, D. W. *Professional Education: Some New Directions.* New York: McGraw-Hill, 1972.

Schmidt, A. M. "Resources for Development of Continuing Education Programs." Paper presented at Conference of Coordinators of Regional Medical Programs, Bethesda, Md., Sept. 30-Oct. 1, 1968.

Schroeder, S., and Haggerty, D. "Competency-Based Individualized Training Programs for Adult Educators: A Nontraditional Approach to Adult Staff Development." In G. Spear (Ed.),

Adult Education Staff Development: Selected Issues, Alternatives, and Implications. Kansas City, Mo.: Center for Resource Development in Adult Education, 1976.

Schroeder, W. L. "Adult Education Defined and Described." In R. M. Smith, G. F. Aker, and J. R. Kidd (Eds.), *Handbook of Adult Education.* New York: Macmillan, 1970.

Seaman, D., and Kohler, E. "Behavioral Skills for Adult Basic Education." Unpublished manuscript, Mississippi Institute for Teacher Training in ABE, Mississippi State University, 1969.

Selltiz, C., Wrightsman, L. S., and Cook, S. W. (Eds.). *Research Methods in Social Relations.* (3rd ed.) New York: Holt, Rinehart and Winston, 1976.

Simon, H. A. *Models of Man.* New York: Wiley, 1957.

Simon, H. A. *Administrative Behavior: A Study of Decision-Making Processes in Administrative Organizations.* (2nd ed.) New York: Macmillan, 1959.

Simon, H. A. *The Sciences of the Artificial.* Cambridge, Mass.: M.I.T. Press, 1969.

Smith, D. "The Determination of Necessary Competencies of Adult Education Administrators and ABE Instructors." Paper presented at Adult Education Research Conference, Minneapolis, April 1977.

Smith, L. M. *The Complexities of an Urban Classroom.* New York: Holt, Rinehart and Winston, 1968.

Smith, R. L. "A Study to Determine the Perceptions of the Competencies Needed by Adult Basic Education Teachers." Unpublished doctoral dissertation, Oregon State University, 1972.

Spangenburg, R. W. *Selecting Methods and Media to Achieve Training Objectives: A Preliminary Manual.* Fort Knox, Ky.: Human Resources Research Organization, 1971.

Stake, R. E. "The Countenance of Educational Evaluation." *Teachers College of Record,* 1967, *68* (7), 523-540.

Stern, M. R. "Compulsory Continuing Education for Professionals or the Gold Rush of '76." In J. S. Long and R. Boshier (Eds.), *Certification, Credentialing, Licensing, and the Renewal Process.* Proceedings of a Conference sponsored by Northwest Adult Education Association, Washington Continuing Education Association, and ERIC Clearinghouse in Career Education. Moscow, Idaho: News Reviews Publishing, 1976.

Stringer, P. "A Rationale for Participation." In N. Cross (Ed.), *Design Participation, Proceedings of the Design Research Society's Conference, Manchester, England, 1971.* London: Academy Editions, 1972.

Stufflebeam, D. L. *Educational Evaluation and Decision Making.* Itasca, Ill.: F. E. Peacock, 1971.

Stuhlmiller, E. M. "The Development and Use of Instruments to Assess the Effectiveness of Paraprofessionals in Working with Low-Income Families." Unpublished doctoral dissertation, Department of Community Service Education, Cornell University, 1973.

Sutton, E. S. "Total Human Resources Development System in AT&T." *Training and Development Journal,* 1977, *31* (1), 4-5.

Synectics Corporation. *Program Performance, 1971: Expanded Food and Nutrition Education Program.* Washington, D.C.: Extension Service, U.S. Department of Agriculture, 1971.

Thompson, J., and McEwen, W. "Organizational Goals and Environment: Goal-Setting as an Interaction Process." In D. Cartwright and A. Zander (Eds.), *Group Dynamics.* (2nd ed.) New York: Harper & Row, 1960.

Thompson, S. "A Field Test of the Model, Design, and Operation of Educative Systems: The Design and Implementation of a Plan of Action to Improve Mutual Consummatory Behavior by Controlling One Component (Interpretations)." Unpublished doctoral dissertation, Program of Postsecondary Education, Florida State University, 1976.

Toffler, A. (Ed.). *Learning for Tomorrow.* New York: Random House, 1974.

Toulmin, S. E., and Baier, K. "On Describing." *Mind,* 1952, *61* (241), 13-38.

Tracey, W. R. *Managing Training and Development Systems.* New York: AMACOM, 1974.

Treffman, S. A. "The Development of Training in Organizations." Paper presented at National Workshop on Extension Staff Development, New Orleans, La., March 1978.

U.S. Department of Agriculture, Extension Service. *Supervising Program Aides in the Expanded Food and Nutrition Education Program.* A supplement to Extension Service Handbook, ESC-574. Washington, D.C.: U.S. Department of Agriculture, 1973.

U.S. Department of Health, Education, and Welfare, Social and Rehabilitation Service. *Research Report No. 3: Overview Study of Employment of Paraprofessionals.* Washington, D.C.: U.S. Government Printing Office, 1974.

U.S. Department of Labor, Manpower Administration. *New Careers, The Community/Home Health Aide.* Trainer's Manual. Washington, D.C.: U.S. Department of Labor, 1968.

University of Chicago. "Teacher Training Conference: Adult Basic Education for Urban Clients." Chicago: Department of Education, University of Chicago, 1972. ED 061 489

University of Missouri, Division for Continuing Education. *ABE National Teacher Training Study, Final Report and Recommendations.* Bethesda, Md.: ERIC Document Reproduction Service, 1973. ED 092 734

University of Southern California. *Institute for Training Adult Education Teachers.* Bethesda, Md.: ERIC Document Reproduction Service, 1970. ED 052 440

Veri, C. C. "Building a Model Doctoral Degree Program in Adult Education." Paper presented at annual meeting of the Professional Training and Development Section of the Adult Education Association of the U.S.A., Atlanta, October 1970.

Verner, C., and others. *The Preparation of Adult Educators: A Selected Review of the Literature Produced in North America.* Syracuse: Adult Education Association of the U.S.A. and the ERIC Clearinghouse on Adult Education, 1970.

Vinter, R. D. "Problems and Processes in Developing Social Work Practice Principles." In E. Thomas (Ed.), *Behavioral Science for Social Workers.* New York: Free Press, 1967.

Vollmer, H. M., and Mills, D. L. *Professionalization.* Englewood Cliffs, N.J.: Prentice-Hall, 1966.

Watkins, B. "Detente in Continuing Education." *Chronicle of Higher Education,* May 14, 1979, p. 6.

"Weather Forecasts: Fair, Gradual Clearing, and Rising Accuracy." *Changing Times,* 1978, *32* (2), 45-47.

Weed, L. L. *Medical Records, Medical Education, and Patient Care: The Problem-Oriented Records as a Basic Tool.* Cleveland, Ohio: Press of Case Western Reserve University, 1969.

Wells, B. B. "The Case Against Mandatory CME." *Virginia Medical Monthly,* April 1977, *104,* 276-279.

"What Life Will Be Like in the 1980s." *U.S. News and World Report,* 1977, *83* (26), 75-86.

Whitlock, G. "Trainer Education and Training." In R. Craig and L. Bittel (Eds.), *Training and Development Handbook.* New York: McGraw-Hill, 1967.

Wilensky, H. L. "The Professionalization of Everyone?" *American Journal of Sociology,* 1964, *70* (2), 137-158.

Wilson, J. *Thinking with Concepts.* Cambridge, England: University Press, 1963.

Wright, J. W. *Human Service Training Project—Final Report.* Ithaca: New York State College of Human Ecology, Cornell University, no date.

Wright, J., and Burmeister, W. *Introduction to Human Services.* Columbus, Ohio: Grid, Inc., 1973.

Yerka, B. L. "Effectiveness of Paraprofessionals in Working with Low-Income Families: An Experimental Study." Unpublished doctoral dissertation, Department of Adult Education, Syracuse University, 1974.

Yura, H., and Walsh, M. B. *The Nursing Process.* (2nd ed.) New York: Appleton-Century-Crofts, 1973.

Zetterberg, H. L. *Social Theory and Social Practice.* New York: Bedminster Press, 1962.

Zetterberg, H. L. *On Theory and Verification in Sociology.* (3rd ed.) New York: Bedminster Press, 1965.

Ziman, J. M. *Public Knowledge: An Essay Concerning the Social Dimension of Science.* London: Cambridge University Press, 1968.

Zinn, L. *Adult Basic Education: Literature Abstracts in Staff Development, 1965-1975.* Kansas City: Center for Resource Development in Adult Education, University of Missouri–Kansas City, 1975.

Index

process of, 100; education related to, 97-99; functions of,
103-104, 109; future of, 128-
132; graduate degree programs
for, 17-38; human resources development related to, xiii, 122,
123-132; issues in, 133-137;
negative image of, 95-98; and organizational development, 104-
109; in organizations, 94-114; of
paraprofessionals, 48-65; for
part-time staff, 39-47; preservice, 1-16; professional continuing education as, 84-93; purposes of, 135; responsibility for,
99-102; and staff development,
103-104; steps in, 119-122; of
volunteers, 66-83
Treffman, S. A., 100, 154

U

U.S. Bureau of Labor Statistics, 84
U.S. Civil Service Commission, 126
U.S. Department of Agriculture,
51, 56, 155
U.S. Department of Education, 9
U.S. Department of Health, Educa-
tion, and Welfare, 55, 57, 59, 155
U.S. Department of Labor, 55, 57,
155
U.S. Office of Economic Opportu-
nity, and paraprofessionals, 61
U.S. Office of Education, 9
Universities. *See* Colleges and uni-
versities

V

Values, levels of, 77-78
Venner, H., 12-13, 146
Veri, C. C., 40, 155
Verner, C., 3, 4, 8, 86, 92, 150, 155
Vinter, R. D., 23, 155
Visalia, California, ABE preservice
training in, 12

Vollmer, H. M., 84, 155
Volunteers: advisory committees
for training of, 68, 82-83; analysis of training for, 66-83; and
categories of organizations, 67-
68; ceremonial activities for, 70-
71; continuing education units
for, 81; evaluating training of,
73-76; group activities for, 72-
73, 78; ideal training program
for, 79-83; individualized training for, 76-79; motivators for,
72; needs assessment for, 68-69;
overview of training methods
for, 68-71; precautions in training of, 73; reinforcement for,
70-71; shift in background of,
67; sociocentricity of, 71-73, 78

W

Walsh, M. B., 23, 156
Watkins, B., 90, 155
Weed, L. L., 23, 156
Wells, B. B., 87, 91, 156
Whitlock, G., 4-5, 156
Wilensky, H. L., 84, 156
Wilson, J., 29, 156
Work Incentive Program (WIN), 127
Workshops, preservice training in,
9
Wright, J. W., 7, 49, 50, 51, 53, 54,
56, 59, 141, 156
Wrightsman, L. S., 28, 153

Y

Yerka, B. L., xv, 48-65, 156
Yura, H., 23, 156

Z

Zetterberg, H. L., 25, 30, 156
Ziman, J. M., 156
Zinn, L., 12, 156